T0353644

# Essential Guides for
# EARLY CAREER TEACHERS

## Teaching Primary Foundation Subjects

# Essential Guides for Early Career Teachers

The *Essential Guides for Early Career Teachers* provide accessible, carefully researched, quick reads for early career teachers. They complement and are fully in line with the new *Early Career Framework* and bring together current information and thinking on each area in one convenient place. The texts are edited by Emma Hollis, Executive Director of NASBTT, who brings a wealth of experience, expertise and knowledge to the series.

# Essential Guides for
# EARLY CAREER
# TEACHERS

## Teaching Primary Foundation Subjects

James Coleman
Series Editor: Emma Hollis

Routledge
Taylor & Francis Group

LONDON AND NEW YORK

NASBTT

First published in 2023 by Critical Publishing Ltd

Published 2025 by Routledge
4 Park Square, Milton Park, Abingdon, Oxon OX14 4RN
605 Third Avenue, New York, NY 10017

Routledge is an imprint of the Taylor & Francis Group, an informa business

British Library Cataloguing in Publication Data
A CIP record for this book is available from the British Library

ISBN: 9781915080899 (pbk)
ISBN: 9781041055501 (ebk)

Cover and text design by Out of House Limited

DOI: 10.4324/9781041055501

# Contents

# Meet the series editor

### Emma Hollis

I am Executive Director of NASBTT (the National Association of School-Based Teacher Trainers) and my absolute passion is teacher education. After gaining a first-class degree in psychology I trained as a primary teacher, and soon became head of initial teacher education for a SCITT provider. I am dedicated to ensuring teachers are given access to high-quality professional development at the early stages of and throughout their careers.

# Meet the author

### James Coleman

I am a primary school teacher and a passionate advocate for the primary foundation subjects. I started my career teaching in inner London schools and led foundation subjects within my first teaching post. Since then, I have been a director of a SCITT in the south of England and now work as Head of Operations and Training at the National Association of School-Based Teacher Training.

# Foreword

As a passionate advocate of high-quality teacher education and continuing professional development, it has always been a source of frustration for me that beyond the Initial Teacher Training year, access to high-quality, structured ongoing professional development has been something of a lottery for teachers. Access and support have been patchy, with some schools and local authorities offering fantastic opportunities for teachers throughout their careers while in other locations CPD has been given lip service at best and, at worst, is non-existent.

This series was conceived of to attempt to close some of those gaps and to offer accessible professional learning to busy teachers in the early stages of their careers. It was therefore a moment of genuine pleasure when proposals for an entitlement for all early career teachers to receive a package of support, guidance and education landed on my desk. There is now a genuine opportunity for school communities to work together to offer the very best early career development for our most precious of resources – the teachers in our schools.

The aim of this series is to distil some of the key topics which occupy an early career teacher's thoughts into digestible, informative texts which will promote discussion, contemplation and reflection and will spark further exploration into practice. In each edition, you will find a series of practical suggestions for how you can put the 'big idea' in each chapter into practice: now, next week and in the long term. By offering opportunities to bring the learning into the classroom in a very concrete way, we hope to help embed many of the principles we share into your day-to-day teaching lives.

All too often, primary teachers find themselves having to make difficult choices when it comes to cramming everything into already over-full days. Foundation subjects can, in some cases, take a back seat as a result of other pressures faced by busy professionals. In this title, James argues a passionate and compelling case for not letting this happen in your classroom. He identifies the challenges faced by early career teachers and suggests practical, usable ways in which you can ensure that a well-rounded curriculum becomes the centrepiece of great teaching in your classroom; offering opportunities for all pupils to excel and recognising the importance of a broad and balanced approach for all.

*Emma Hollis*
Executive Director, NASBTT

# Chapter 1    Why foundation subjects?

## What? (The big idea)

### Valuing foundation subjects

> *If a curriculum cannot change, move, perturb, inform teachers, it will have no effect on those whom they teach. It must be first and foremost a curriculum for teachers. If it has any effect on pupils, it will have it by virtue of having had an effect on teachers.*
>
> (Bruner, 1977)

It would be fair to say that the modern-day teacher has a lot on their plate. Whether it's worrying about statutory assessments, marking books or Ofsted visits among the daily splitting of priorities and energy that teachers face, far too often it is the foundation subjects that are pushed to the very back of their thinking. This book has been created to try and persuade you that foundation subjects are not only worth your full attention but are vital if you want the children in your classes to reach their true potential in life. That wonderful performance on the West End stage wouldn't happen without the teacher who ignited a passion for music and drama at primary school. The lifesaving technology within our modern cars may not have been created without the chance to build a birdbox in Year 2. Our Olympic, Paralympic and other sporting heroes wouldn't exist if it wasn't for the opportunity to refine and develop skills during PE lessons at school.

It's true that the idea of teaching fundamental movement skills in a school hall, covered in peas left over after lunch, might not be the most appealing prospect for a lot of teachers. But it's not about the teachers. No. You owe it to the children you are responsible for teaching to give them these opportunities. How can you create the next Mo Farah if you don't let them run? The next Nadiya Hussain if you don't bake? A generation to finally solve global warming if you don't teach geography? Foundation subjects are more than words on a national curriculum document. They represent passion, dreams, and careers. A curriculum's ultimate goal should be to reflect and prepare pupils for the modern and diverse society in which they will live and work. Your starting point needs to be who is this curriculum for and once you are clear on that point, what knowledge and skills do your students require in order to thrive?

Foundation subjects can't be discussed without considering how these are defined as being 'foundation'. The national curriculum is the starting point and driver for nearly everything that is taught within classrooms. The most recent version, created in 2014, states that its aim is to:

> provide pupils with an introduction to the essential knowledge they need to be educated citizens. It introduces pupils to the best that has been thought and said, and helps engender an appreciation of human creativity and achievement.

(DfE, 2014)

How often are teachers introduced to this section of the national curriculum, rather than the far drier 'programme of study'? The very best teachers delicately balance the statutory elements of the national curriculum with this far wider aim of ensuring children become the citizens of tomorrow that you would want them to be. In simple terms, if your class cannot only recall the key figures and dates involved in the Battle of Hastings but also understand the cause and consequence of the Anglo-Saxon era ending and what lessons there might be for us to learn in the modern world, you are meeting all expectations of the national curriculum. You'll also have a group of children who are enthusiastic, passionate and excited to learn. Facts without context are like individuals without society. The foundation subjects are too often watered down to a worksheet and fact gathering. This is completely unnecessary, as is explored throughout the pages of this book.

There is an unhealthy narrative that says English and mathematics are taking attention away from the foundation subjects. Try being an engineer without understanding basic mathematics. How about being an actor without the ability to read with expression and intonation? English and mathematics teach children vital skills that are transferable and fundamental to everyday life. Teaching these subjects well, and in depth, on a frequent basis is not a bad thing. However, the *entire* curriculum being taught effectively is what creates grounded, intelligent and ultimately successful children. Learning breeds confidence and confidence breeds learning. People all have unique and specific strengths. A curriculum that is narrow and only values the strengths of a small number of subjects can leave a large number of children lost in a cycle of what feels like a never-ending failure. It's amazing how success in one subject can create a domino effect of success across the curriculum. Adults wouldn't choose to only engage in subjects or activities they don't enjoy. It is unfair to force the same principle on the children within schools.

It's important to state at this point that no book, continuing professional development (CPD) programme or website will give you everything you will ever need to know about a curriculum subject. Your own subject knowledge will never stop growing and nor will it ever be complete. That's why feeling empowered and knowing where to get high-quality support is so important to an early career teacher. The reality is that most primary teachers are a 'jack of all trades' and will need to be able to know a little about a lot, rather than be an expert in one or two areas. At 10:45 you might be inspiring young minds about the most efficient way to multiply three-digit numbers and then by 14:00 you are dressed as a Viking dissecting why groups throughout history have been obsessed with power. In order to have this breadth of knowledge, you will need to be self-motivated and, importantly, informed about where to go for support. The final part of this book will list subject associations for you to make contact with. These fantastic organisations should be your first port of call for support, far more so than Google or any other internet search engines. Not that they don't have their place, they do; it's just that you shouldn't assume the top result on a search engine is the most effective tool for supporting children's learning.

The hope is that by the end of this book, you not only feel like you have the skills and strategies to teach foundation subjects effectively, but you also passionately believe that each child within your class deserves the opportunity to discover their own unique interests and skills. It's hard to think of many jobs as rewarding or important as that of being a teacher. Every time you stand in front of a class of children, you are in a position of extreme privilege and opportunity. Ensuring that the children in your classes have the opportunity to engage in an entire curriculum is not only your duty, but something to celebrate and embrace.

# So what?

This book has been written in the aftermath of a global pandemic. As a consequence of the incredibly challenging choices that schools and teachers had to make in reference to the curriculum, foundation subjects are being pushed further and further to the periphery of our thinking. It is not unreasonable to think that a trainee teacher could go through their entire training year without having had any experience of teaching certain subjects. It is obvious that there are numerous issues that come with the situation we find ourselves in but, in my opinion, the biggest challenge is that lots of teachers won't be able to see the huge impact effective planning and teaching of foundation subjects can have on pupil progress. In truth, the pandemic has only exacerbated an existing problem. School timetables are often heavily weighted in favour of the core subjects, leaving very little opportunity for trainee and early career teachers to teach foundation subjects. This in turn creates teachers who are less likely to value these subjects and the vicious cycle continues. This chapter explores how attitudes towards the foundation subjects can and do have a profound impact on the quality of learning and progress children make.

The book unpicks what it is that makes high-quality teaching within foundation subjects and allows you to think in the same way an experienced teacher would. It starts with the basics and works its way up, until you have all the tools necessary to teach the foundation subjects feeling empowered and confident.

One of the main issues for teachers is that even when a geography, history or modern foreign languages lesson is timetabled to be taught, the planning process is rarely valued as much as it should be.

* Analyse your planning, preparation and assessment (PPA) time and consider how much of that time is given over to planning foundation subjects. It's likely to not be all that much, yet it will probably form at least half of your teaching time during the week. As outlined later on, there are plenty of completely legitimate reasons for this. This is not an exercise to make you feel guilty or like you're doing a bad job. Complete Table 1.1 to help you with this task.

**Table 1.1  Planning PPA time**

| Subject | Time in minutes | Percentage of your PPA |
|---|---|---|
| Planning English | | |
| Planning mathematics | | |
| Planning foundation subjects | | |
| Assessing English | | |
| Assessing mathematics | | |
| Assessing foundation subjects | | |
| Activities not related to lesson planning/assessments | | |

This task provides a picture of just how much time you devote to foundation subjects as part of your planning and assessment cycle. It's likely that half of each timetabled day will be handed over to these subjects. Are you comfortable with the amount of time you spend planning and assessing them or does the balance seem too heavily weighted one way or another? The likelihood is that you will be spending a disproportionate amount of time on the core subjects, perhaps neglecting the foundation subjects. This, in a lot of ways, is not a surprise. We currently operate in a school system that directly judges school performance against Year 6 SATs results; tests that only focus on English, mathematics and, for some, science. This has meant we are often left with a school curriculum heavily focused on these subjects to try and improve end of Year 6 outcomes. As this book has already started to unpick, in order for children to grow and make progress across all areas of the curriculum, it is vital they are given ample opportunity to do so.

## Case study ◀◀◀

### A broad and balanced approach

*When I first started teaching, my focus was relentlessly on maths and English. My attitude had been that if over half of my teaching timetable was to be teaching these subjects, then it makes sense for me to get those subjects right before worrying about the rest. Looking back, I know why I did this, but it is only with experience that I have learnt the negative impact this had on not only my own development but that of the children in my class.*

*A broad and balanced curriculum offering for children allows everyone in class the opportunity to 'tap into' things that they are passionate about. I know as an adult that when I am confident in something, that can then feed into other aspects of my life. If I spent each day relentlessly focusing on the same things every day, I would quickly become uninspired and disengaged. By ensuring each subject of the curriculum was included in my fortnightly timetable, I kept things fresh and interesting for all of us in class, but I also saw the potential of every child. Children who might have struggled in one subject shone in another. The impact wasn't just academic; breaking down some of the children's unhealthy perceptions of each other as learners meant that different relationships formed in class. Those who might normally be supporting others were now the novice. It allowed the dynamic to shift and a refreshing respect to grow between different groups of children. This filtered into playground behaviour being more positive and cliques being broken down.*

*It was intimidating to start with and it felt overwhelming to try to spread myself evenly across each curriculum subject. I relied on the support of colleagues, subject leads within school and my partner teacher to lead me through the challenges. They recommended high-quality resources for me to engage with and upskill myself when I needed to. I hadn't thought about the French language since my GCSEs, so it was intimidating to think I had to teach it to little people. However, it was scarier when I went into lessons feeling unprepared. There is nothing worse than feeling fraudulent in the front of the class and the children feel it too. Asking for help and support made me a better teacher and, just as importantly, allowed me to enjoy teaching the subject. The old adage of 'the more you put in, the more you get back' has followed me around during my teaching career.*

*As an early career teacher, you have a lot to focus on and you understandably want to get the basics right. Looking back on my career, I wish that, the second I had nailed the basics, I had ensured my classroom was inclusive of every subject across the curriculum. Not only would it have supported my development as a teacher, but it would have made a huge difference for my class. Both academically and socially.*

# Now what? ◀ ◀ ◀

## Practical task for tomorrow ◀ ◀ ◀

- Using Table 1.1 that you completed earlier, plan your PPA sessions to include dedicated time for foundation subjects. How much time you can spare will depend on your individual circumstance, but start off small and build from there.

- After a month of implementing this new schedule, review its impact on both the outcomes for children and your own confidence in teaching these subjects.

## Practical task for next week ◀ ◀ ◀

- Consider which subjects you feel most confident in and the subjects in which you'd like to develop your knowledge.

- Once you have identified these, arrange a meeting with the subject co-ordinator within the school and ask for support to help build your confidence.

- Ask your colleague where the content for the curriculum has come from and how it has been developed over time. This will allow you to identify key concepts to focus on and hopefully make the task of teaching the subject a little less intimidating.

## Practical task for the longer term ◀ ◀ ◀

It may seem like a long time away but it won't take long before you are taking responsibility for a foundation subject within your school. Primary schools have a lot of subjects and not that many teachers and so it comes to pass that within the first few years, you will likely be planning across a wider remit than just your class. Start to consider the subjects you would like to explore further and consider asking your school for some CPD within that area. Not only is professional development proven to keep teachers in their careers, but it will also allow you to become more of an expert in one area, which opens up career pathways as you move through school.

# What next?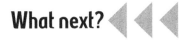

## Further reading

Allison, S and Tharby, A (2015) *Make Every Lesson Count*. Carmarthen: Crown House.

Lemov, D (2015) *Teach Like a Champion*. San Francisco: Jossey-Bass.

Sherrington, T (2019) *Rosenshine's Principles in Action*. Woodbridge: John Catt Educational Ltd.

Sherrington, T and Caviglioli, O (2020) *Teaching WalkThrus*. Woodbridge: John Catt Educational Ltd.

## References

Bruner, J (1977) *The Process of Education*. Cambridge, MA: Harvard University Press.

Department for Education (2014) *The National Curriculum*. [online] Available at: www.gov.uk/national-curriculum/key-stage-1-and-2 (accessed 12 December 2022).

# Chapter 2　Jack of all trades? Foundation subject knowledge for teachers

## What? (The big idea)

### Knowing that you can't know it all

*Teachers must know the subject they teach. Indeed, there may be nothing more foundational to teacher competency. The reason is simple: Teachers who do not themselves know a subject well are not likely to have the knowledge they need to help students learn this content.*

(Ball et al, 2008)

There are eight foundation subjects. It's rare to come across anybody who will be just as informed on cross-sectional and exploded diagrams in design and technology as they are in biomes and vegetation belts in geography. If you are, can I suggest you apply to a TV gameshow and earn yourself an excellent pay day? The point is you don't need to be an expert to teach each foundation subject effectively. Of course, you need to know about the subject you are teaching and spend sufficient time familiarising yourself with the content to be able to address misconceptions and identify key outcomes for pupils. However, it is unreasonable, unrealistic and ultimately, if you teach and plan effectively, unnecessary to be an expert in every subject. The way you teach a subject is as important as the content you are delivering. How do you teach more than just the facts and figures? How do you inspire, excite and, ultimately, develop a lifelong love for a subject? It requires more than just a PowerPoint and worksheet.

This chapter looks at two different types of subject knowledge that you might want to develop for each foundation subject: substantive and disciplinary knowledge. Recognising the difference between substantive knowledge and disciplinary knowledge within each subject can have a profound impact on your understanding of a subject and, consequently, on how you might teach that subject.

» **Substantive knowledge** is the content that teachers teach as established fact. You might want pupils to know about crotchets, percentages, the Treaty of Versailles or Debussy. In calling this 'substantive', the material presented is treated as a given or fact.

» **Disciplinary knowledge**, by contrast, is a curricular term for what pupils learn about how that knowledge was established. Using the Treaty of Versailles as an example, the date it was established is a given. Many events before and after the Treaty of Versailles are givens. But attributions of cause, consequence or significance to the Treaty of Versailles are not givens and this is the disciplinary knowledge. This is where there is an opportunity for you to engage in debate, challenge thinking and develop skills for pupils.

Put simply, a teacher with sound disciplinary knowledge can help pupils make sense of the substantive knowledge. Facts without context can feel intimidating, aimless and it can be very hard to retain the information. Equally, context without facts leaves children confused without the factual knowledge to understand why something might be important or profound. Ultimately, a teacher who only develops and feels confident about their substantive knowledge, the facts, is likely to fail to inspire the children that they are teaching within their classroom, so ideally you need to find a blend between the two.

## Reflective task ◀◀◀

Let's consider an example to help define the differences between substantive and disciplinary knowledge. For this example, we are going to use the Key Stage 2 geography curriculum and particularly the strand relating to 'human geography, including: types of settlement and land use, economic activity including trade links, and the distribution of natural resources including energy, food, minerals and water' (DfE, 2013). A school might choose to look at a local city to study types of settlement. For the sake of this task, we'll use London. Table 2.1 outlines the different types of knowledge that you would want to blend together in order to give pupils a holistic view of the subject and, as a consequence, a deeper understanding.

Table 2.1 Substantive and disciplinary knowledge

| Substantive knowledge | Disciplinary knowledge |
|---|---|
| City | Why cities are built where they are. |
| London | Common features of cities (often near rivers, etc). |
| Population of 9 million | |
| South-East of England | Why do we need cities, towns and villages? |
| Capital of England | What is the purpose of a city? |
| European capital city | Why are buildings in London often different to the ones that are built in small towns or villages? |
| River Thames | |
| Parliament | |
| Tower of London | |
| Urban | |
| Rural | |

This is clearly not an exhaustive list and you may choose to focus on other facts, vocabulary and talking points in your own context. However, the table does illustrate just how important it is to have both substantive and disciplinary knowledge present within your foundation subject planning. In isolation, a child being able to tell someone that 9 million people live in London is not of much use. A child being able to tell someone that 9 million people live in London and understand *why* such a large number live there is a whole different matter. The disciplinary knowledge of understanding that big cities are often full of industry and opportunities for employment helps contextualise the facts for pupils. Many pupils may know that the River Thames flows through London. Will they know that Paris has the Seine, Rome has the Tiber and Budapest has the Danube? Understanding that most big cities were created hundreds of years ago because rivers were a life source providing water and irrigation to produce food allows children to see similarities and make links between different countries and the development of society across thousands of years.

This approach can be applied to any foundation subject you are teaching. Design and technology is about more than being able to design and build a product. Pupils need to consider why products are made in the real world. Is it useful? Does it solve a problem that exists? Would it be a successful product and why? Is it cost-effective? There's no point designing a beautiful chocolate teapot, as fun and delicious as that may be.

Knowing how to order a croissant and coffee with milk may be a useful skill for an eight-year-old, but understanding how a language has come to be is just as, if not more, useful. Being able to identify and understand the links between different languages is going to deepen a child's understanding and therefore make them more likely to continue learning a language in the future. So when you are talking to them about breakfast on the Cote d'Azur, also ask them to consider where they think the words cliché, liaison or déjà vu derive from.

There are examples across every single subject in the national curriculum. The way mathematics is taught in schools has developed along similar lines of thinking. Perhaps 20 years ago, it was enough to be able to use the column method to solve addition problems and not *understand* the mathematical concepts. It is now widely accepted that this is not going to be enough if we want our pupils to really understand numbers and some of the concepts that link different operations together.

» Rules and methods: substantive knowledge.

» Connecting big ideas and links between different areas of mathematics: disciplinary knowledge.

To have one without the other means learning is inevitably not as deep as it needs to be. A high-quality curriculum ensures pupils learn both the substantive knowledge required to connect prior learning with new, as well as the disciplinary knowledge which leads to pupils connecting learning between subject domains.

One of my favourite quotes related to teaching is from a man called Haim Ginott: *'It's my daily mood that makes the weather. As a teacher I possess tremendous power to make a child's life miserable or joyous'*. This is obviously linked to our wider roles within school but I think it is just as true when looking through the lens of subject knowledge. When talking about this, I always refer to my school experience. I took GCSE history and absolutely loved it. My teacher made me feel like the subject was alive and his enthusiasm and energy inspired me. As a result, I chose history as one of my A levels. Within four weeks, I had dropped it for another subject. The big difference was the teacher. The subject content hadn't changed – the substantive knowledge – the facts and figures weren't any different but the pedagogical approach and, importantly, the disciplinary knowledge that had been valued so greatly by my previous teacher were no longer there. We were learning about facts without the opportunity to debate meaning or consider consequence in a meaningful way. To relate it back to the previous quote, my GCSE history teacher made the weather feel like I was sitting on the beach in glorious wall-to-wall sunshine and 30-degree heat and my A level teacher made me feel like I was sitting at the bus stop, without a shelter, in the sort of rain that clings to your clothes.

# So what?

As a teacher, you hold incredible influence over the children you teach. It is the privilege of a lifetime but also a huge responsibility – not one to shy away from but to embrace and enjoy. The choices you make in relation to the knowledge you focus on during lessons have a direct impact on the progress of the children. It sounds obvious but how often do you really consider what content you are teaching? Do you consider the balance of substantive and disciplinary knowledge, and the power you have to balance these, when you access last year's planning or open the scheme of work your school has purchased? If you only chose to teach facts and figures, the children in your class will only learn facts and figures. If you chose not to talk about cause and consequence in history, then the children in your class won't understand why it's important or how to deal with these issues in their own lives. If you don't talk to the children about the differences in techniques and practices across different crafts in art and design, then your children won't know there is a choice. It's simple but powerful. You have a duty to ensure that the children you are responsible for nurturing and supporting towards their dreams are given the opportunity to do so. By considering what knowledge you want them to explore, question and enquire about, you are ensuring that you can hold your head up high knowing you taught something you thought was important.

## Case study ◀◀◀

### Understanding the concept of concepts

*Joe Haysom – Foundation Subjects Co-ordinator*

*Leading a foundation subject within school has been a steep learning curve for me but a responsibility I have really enjoyed. My experience tells me that early career teachers can find the prospect of teaching foundation subjects quite intimidating. This is totally understandable given the breadth of knowledge that you could teach within each subject. The key is to narrow this wide range of possibilities to some key concepts that are teachable across a variety of topics. If a school is able to identify those key concepts that make up the fascinating parts of each subject and create a curriculum that focuses on only those concepts, then the learning becomes really clear for both teacher and learners. Knowing that nearly all war comes about from the desire to have more power can give children a far deeper understanding of a range of historical events than being able to recall the timeline of the Romans. Making links between human settlements and nature's resources allows learners to take their understanding and apply it to new contexts.*

*The key to being able to teach this effectively is ensuring the concepts that are being taught are explicit in both the teacher and learner's mind. This requires a strong curriculum that has identified these concepts and ensured they are threaded through each subject across age phases. As an early career teacher, this is not your responsibility, but you can do a lot to help yourself on the journey to becoming more confident with teaching foundation subjects.*

*During my first few years in teaching, I used some of my PPA time to work alongside subject leaders within my school. I would ask them to highlight what they thought the key concepts of their subject were. By doing this, I was able to look at each subject and each lesson plan through the lens of these key concepts. I ensured that I made links to these concepts explicit during conversations with the children and during my teaching. The impact was profound. Having common concepts to return to for each subject, no matter what topic we were covering, meant there was consistency and clarity. What was once intimidating and complex became far simpler and empowered me to teach across the curriculum with confidence.*

# Now what? ◀ ◀ ◀

## Practical task for tomorrow ◀ ◀ ◀

In the same way that you explored earlier, look at your foundation subject planning and begin to identify the types of knowledge that you think is prevalent. Is there a good balance between substantive and disciplinary knowledge? Are you happy with the content that has been planned? Which key themes can you pick out that you would want the children to focus on? Use the following template to support you with this task.

| Substantive knowledge | Disciplinary knowledge |
|---|---|
| *Look at the subject you are teaching. What are the key bits of vocabulary that you want the children to learn?* <br><br> *What are the key facts and figures? Any key figures or names for the children to be aware of?* | *What key concepts can you pick out? Are there issues that can contribute to rich debate and discussion?* <br><br> *How can you deepen children's understanding of the subject?* <br><br> *How is the substantive knowledge established?* <br><br> *How do the children feel about the subject?* |
| **Example of key themes to explore** | |
| *Just because King Henry VIII was a bad husband, does that make him a bad king?* | |
| *If people who live in cities have higher salaries, why doesn't everyone want to live in a city?* | |
| *Why might it be valuable for members of a society to belong to a faith community?* | |
| *Why would we want to create multiple prototypes before creating the final version of a product?* | |

## Practical task for next week ◀ ◀ ◀

Look at the topics you are covering within your foundation subjects at the moment. Can you break down the topics into different types of knowledge? To get you started, use the examples within this chapter: substantive and disciplinary knowledge. How will you ensure children understand both? What strategies or activities might you use for either one and how does your pedagogical approach change?

## Practical task for the longer term ◀◀◀

Join as many subject associations as you possibly can. It's an incredibly simple task but one that will have a profound impact on your practice and ability to teach across the curriculum. You want to avoid the gamble of using an internet search engine to support you when planning lessons. Subject associations not only have CPD and events for you to attend but also a wide range of online resources that you can use to support every aspect of your role. There is often a nominal fee associated with membership, or you can speak to your school about applying for an organisation membership.

# What next? ◀ ◀ ◀

## Further reading

Bailin, S, Case, R, Coombs, J R and Daniels, L B (1999) Common Misconceptions of Critical Thinking. *Journal of Curriculum Studies*, 31(3): 269–83.

Coe, R, Aloisi, C, Higgins, S and Major, L E (2014) *What Makes Great Teaching: Review of the Underpinning Research*. Durham University. [online] Available at: http://bit.ly/2OvmvKO (accessed 12 December 2022).

Education Endowment Foundation (2017) Metacognition and Self-regulated Learning Guidance Report. [online] Available at: https://educationendowmentfoundation.org.uk/tools/guidance-reports (accessed 12 December 2022).

Education Endowment Foundation (2018) Sutton Trust–Education Endowment Foundation Teaching and Learning Toolkit. [online] Available at: https://educationendowmentfoundation.org.uk/evidence-summaries/teaching-learning-toolkit (accessed 12 December 2022).

## References

Ball, D L, Thames, M H and Phelps, G (2008) Content Knowledge for Teachers: What Makes It Special? *Journal of Teacher Education*, 59: 389–407. [online] Available at: www.math.ksu.edu/~bennett/onlinehw/qcenter/ballmkt.pdf (accessed 12 December 2022).

Department for Education (DfE) (2013*) History Programmes of Study: Key Stages 1 and 2*. [online] Available at: https://assets.publishing.service.gov.uk/government/uploads/system/uploads/attachment_data/file/239035/PRIMARY_national_curriculum_-_History.pdf (accessed 12 December 2022).

Ginott, H G (1993) *Teacher and Child: A Book for Parents and Teachers*. Hoboken, NJ: Prentice Hall and IBD.

# Chapter 3    Subject knowledge for pupils

## What? (The big idea)

### Keeping things simple

*The act of retrieving learning from memory has two profound benefits. One, it tells you what you know and don't know, and therefore where to focus further study to improve the areas where you're weak. Two, recalling what you have learned causes your brain to reconsolidate the memory, which strengthens its connections to what you already know and makes it easier for you to recall in the future.*

(Brown et al, 2014)

Taking responsibility for your very own class in September is both terrifying and exhilarating at the same time. You have your very own group of little people staring back at you six hours a day, waiting to be modelled into the society of tomorrow. You will have a million and one fears and dreams that you will want to move past and impact on. After the first few 'deer in the headlights' months, you get to a point of understanding your role far better, and the focus will shift away from your day-to-day teaching and more to your planning and assessment of the children's learning. The cramped nature of the primary curriculum has already been discussed.

When you only have, at best, an hour for a subject each week, what you choose to teach becomes even more important. The temptation can be to try and counteract this lack of opportunity to teach the subject as often as we might like by cramming in as many different topics as possible within each subject. We have all become comfortable discussing the depth at which children understand core subjects, especially within maths. The idea that subject matter needs to be covered more than once and, vitally, from more than just one angle is accepted as being important to help children understand numbers and maths more generally. For rich, deep and meaningful learning, this logic needs to be applied to all the subjects you teach. Teaching fewer things in greater depth is not only what is best for the children in your class but it is also infinitely more enjoyable for you as a practitioner. The opportunity to immerse yourself and your class in a specific period of history over the course of a half term can lead to some incredible discussions, debates, ideas and, most importantly, powerful learning. Learning that lasts and inspires. Understanding requires an iterative mix of experiences, reflections on those experiences and targeted instruction in light of those experiences. Good lesson design is reliant on the provision of sufficiently real or simulated experiences in order to enable pupils' understanding to develop. It is your job, the teacher, to equip and enable pupils to eventually perform with understanding and increasing autonomy. That is quite different from preparing them for a test or worrying about curriculum coverage.

To do this, teachers should ask themselves: what kinds of knowledge, skills and routines are prerequisites for a successful pupil outcome? What kinds of tasks and activities will help the class develop and deepen their understanding of key ideas? And so, when planning lessons, you should aim to cover less curriculum content but to cover that content in greater depth. You should provide opportunities for pupils to explore the subject matter from a range of perspectives and to provide sufficient experience and context.

# So what?

Back to the worksheets – the idea that children need to be engaged in a subject or topic for a substantial amount of time means there is a responsibility on teachers to ensure they plan engaging and meaningful opportunities to enquire, explore and debate issues. The title of this chapter is related to the subject knowledge of pupils but it is impossible to talk about a pupil's subject knowledge without first considering your own.

It's important to reiterate the belief that you by no means need to be an expert in every single subject in order to teach it effectively. You absolutely need to be an expert in understanding *how* children learn effectively and then use this knowledge to support and supplement your specific subject knowledge. I am a terrible artist. Truly awful, and I know nothing about how to paint, draw, design; the list could go on until we ran out of ink. My lack of knowledge meant I had to learn how to do these things. I was still not an expert. However, my new knowledge, supported by my clear understanding of how I wanted to teach the children in my class, was more than enough to ensure some incredibly rich learning opportunities during our art lessons.

This mistaken idea that teachers have to be an expert in every subject they teach is a demotivating and high-pressured expectation. You need to be an expert in your children. You need to be an expert in knowing how to engage them in a subject. You need to be an expert in identifying the 'big ideas' from a subject and engaging children in meaningful enquiry, learning and experiences related to these themes that you have skilfully identified and learnt about. Big ideas are not necessarily taught directly but are built from small ideas linked together. They are sometimes described as 'powerful' because they have greater explanatory power in helping learners to understand the world. Identifying the nature of progression from small to big ideas is central to setting out what pupils should be learning at various points as they move through their school years. Mary Myatt (2020) states if a child understands a 'big idea' then new material around that becomes much stickier and is easier to make sense of. Let's consider an example; you might focus on the Key Stage 1 geography national curriculum, which asks you to:

*understand geographical similarities and differences through studying the human and physical geography of a small area of the UK and of a small area in a contrasting non-European country.*

(DfE, 2014)

The big idea you want to focus on might be how humans have adapted to survive in different geographical environments but to understand that, you would need to start much smaller. Your first lesson might look at the geography of your local area in the UK. Chances are it will be relatively green, a climate that is relatively mild throughout the year and without extreme weather patterns. With that in mind, the houses will be designed and built to withstand very few extreme weather events. You might want to then look at villages and towns that have been built in Siberia. Remember, try not to just focus on how they are different but on why they are different. You'll want the children to start to consider the 'big idea' of survival. Humankind's relationship with nature is a delicate one. The world around us has been designed to allow us to survive and thrive and it is very specific to the geography of that part of the world. Houses in Siberia are markedly different to the houses built in the UK. A young child would look at the two types of houses and might well assume that once you have identified they are different, that's the end of the story. Not so. The key concept is that, actually, they are exactly the same. Your house is built to a specification that will keep you most safe in your environment. The same goes for the wooden lodge in Serbia, an igloo in Antarctica or a clay Kutcha house in the Sahara. They all look very different, but the key concept is that they are all built and designed for one purpose – to keep humans safe. This deeper learning and discussion will allow the children in your class to understand the world around them in a way that broadens horizons, sparks curiosity and generates further questions to be answered. These 'big ideas' or concepts are talked about in more detail later in the book.

In order to understand exactly what the children in your class need to understand, you need to be familiar with your own school's curriculum. It is highly likely that each subject at your school will have a member of staff who is responsible for the development of the curriculum. Conversations with experienced colleagues can be some of the most enlightening you will have during the early stages of your careers. Book in some time with the lead of the subject that you'd like to understand better and ask for their advice. Some key questions that you can ask for each subject are listed below.

## Reflective task ◄◄◄

- What are the common misconceptions for children at this age within this subject?

- How does the school curriculum build on knowledge across year groups?

- What has been covered in the year before the one that I am teaching and what will be covered in the year after? (Remember, don't just focus on the topics being covered but the 'big ideas' and concepts.)

- What planning is already in place? Where does this planning come from?

- How do we record the children's work when teaching foundation subjects?

- What does assessment look like in this subject? Can you show me some examples?

By having these discussions with those responsible for subject leadership, you will be able to plan engaging sequences of lessons that are not only going to benefit the children in your class but will support their development over time as they move through the different stages of school. This joined-up thinking and planning between year groups is crucial if you want to ensure children's knowledge is being built upon in a coherent and effective way.

## Case study ◄◄◄

### Needing to know what they already know

*Sian Rodgers – Key Stage 2 teacher*

*One of the things I remember most clearly from my training year was this feeling of intimidation when observing my mentor teaching. It all looked so easy. I would be struggling to get the children quiet on the carpet during my lessons, while my mentor seemed to have everyone and everything on a string. One of the most important areas of my practice that I wanted to improve was the ability to address misconceptions the children had. I really struggled to see them during whole class teaching and my subject knowledge wasn't secure enough to be able to address them at the time of them arising within taught lessons. I knew I needed to address this blind spot in my teaching if I wanted to feel more confident at the front of the class and support the learners in making progress. But without the benefit of experience in teaching a year group, I struggled to* understand how I would gain this knowledge. My mentor suggested I speak with an experienced teacher from the year group I was teaching in before starting my planning and asking them for the key areas of misconception that they knew the children would have. Their experience of having taught something multiple times to multiple classes meant that this teacher was able to tell me, ahead of it happening, what the children would struggle to understand. This was a pivotal moment for me in my teaching career. I had always focused my energy on ensuring I knew what subject knowledge I needed to know and had never considered what I needed to know about the children's understanding of that subject. Of course, every child and class is different and so you can't always predict exactly what misconceptions might crop up. But within each subject and each year group, there are some key misconceptions that learners will always stumble over.

So, what impact did pre-empting these misconceptions have on me as a practitioner? The main thing was that I felt far more prepared and confident to 'dive' into the problem with the children. Rather than panicking when someone had got something wrong and worrying that I wouldn't be able to support that child to the answer because I had been caught off guard, I would have already known the issue that would crop up and therefore be able to deal with the issue on the spot. The power of being able to identify and address a problem as and when it occurs is massive and has a profound impact on the progress of the children. The main thing it gave me was confidence. Confidence to plan and deliver lessons that focused on the right things and allowed me to be nimble and able to adapt to the understanding of the class.

## Reflective task ◀◀◀

1. What are the implications for you as an early career teacher?

2. What can you learn from this to further your development?

3. What one thing will you do differently as a consequence of this case study?

# Now what? ◀ ◀ ◀

## Practical task for tomorrow ◀◀◀

Teaching involves at least two people. There is always more than one perspective and it's important that you consider how the children in your class are interacting with your teaching. Use one of your foundation subject lessons to ask the children what they have learnt so far during the topic. Do their answers reflect what you were expecting? Have they been aware of what success looked like or have they missed the purpose of what was being taught? By having these relaxed opportunities to assess how your class is interacting with your teaching, you can adapt and be flexible in a very live sense, rather than having to wait until marking books before making changes.

## Practical task for next week ◀◀◀

Take a look at the planning and workbooks for the year groups either side of the one you are teaching. Have a look at what the expectations are and what is being covered so that you can see where the children have come from and where they are expected to be next year. Discuss content coverage with your fellow teachers and then reflect on what you have seen. Based on the outcomes of this exercise, start to feed your conclusions into your planning and teaching. This will allow you to ensure that you are not only aware of what you are teaching for the here and now but also what knowledge to build on and what knowledge the class will need to continue to thrive. It's important to remember that children learn best when they are able to revisit knowledge across different subjects and with varied contexts. Simply giving children knowledge during a lesson, asking them to carry out a task and then never revisiting this knowledge again will not result in long-term learning. Ensuring that your planning is linked to and builds upon learning that has already taken place allows you to ensure this deep learning occurs across all subjects in the curriculum.

## Practical task for the longer term ◀◀◀

Speak to your school to see what links they have with other schools. Once you have identified an appropriate school, work alongside a teacher in the same year group as you to discuss your approaches to teaching foundation subjects. Look at children's work together and compare the quality of outcome. Try your best to be open-minded and not see it as a judgement of each other's practice. Instead, see it as a valuable opportunity to learn from each other and consider a perspective you may not have thought about. Teachers are very used to formal moderation processes when working with colleagues in other schools. An informal but professional discussion can be just as fruitful for both you and the children you teach.

# What next? ◀◀◀

## Further reading

Allen, B and Sims, S (2018) *The Teacher Gap*. Abingdon: Routledge.

Black, P and Wiliam, D (2009) Developing the Theory of Formative Assessment. *Educational Assessment, Evaluation and Accountability*, 21(1): 5–31.

Clark, R, Nguyen, F and Sweller, J (2006) *Efficiency in Learning: Evidence-Based Guidelines to Manage Cognitive Load*. San Francisco, CA: John Wiley & Sons.

Hattie, J (2012) *Visible Learning for Teachers*. London: Routledge.

Willingham, D T (2009) *Why Don't Students Like School?* San Francisco, CA: Jossey-Bass.

## References

Brown, P, Roediger, H and McDaniel, M (2014) *Make it Stick: The Science of Successful Learning*. Cambridge, MA: Harvard University Press.

Department for Education (DfE) (2014) *Geography Programmes of Study: Key Stages 1 and 2*. [online] Available at: https://assets.publishing.service.gov.uk/government/uploads/system/uploads/attachment_data/file/239044/PRIMARY_national_curriculum_-_Geography.pdf (accessed 12 December 2022).

Myatt, M (2020) Concepts. [online] Available at: www.marymyatt.com/blog/concepts (accessed 12 December 2022).

# Chapter 4   Making an impact: understanding subject concepts

## What? (The big idea)

### Focus on the concepts

*Content, therefore, is important, not as facts to be memorised... but because without it students cannot acquire concepts and, therefore, will not develop their understanding and progress in their learning.*

(Young et al, 2014)

One of the biggest challenges for teachers, especially those in the first few years of their career, is knowing what to focus on when teaching subjects. The national curriculum gives us a very useful scaffold from which to build but even within specific subjects there is an almost overwhelming amount of choice. Judaism – do I focus on key religious figures? How Judaism came to be? The challenging history Jews have faced throughout the years? This list could be added to almost indefinitely and so the challenge is obvious – what do teachers choose to teach their pupils? This is where key concepts can be incredibly helpful and the importance of your school having an integrated curriculum becomes apparent.

Cambridge Assessment International Education summarises where some of the earliest thinking and research around curriculum concepts took place.

*Concept formation is an area of research in psychology. It refers to how people acquire or learn to use concepts. In the* 'Big Book of Concepts', *Gregory Murphy summarises research in this area of psychology. Concept formation traces the way people develop an understanding of their experience, what systems of categorisation they develop, and how they learn and use these systems. This research often focuses on concepts of fairly basic, concrete things, for example, types of animals and their features.*

(Cambridge Assessment International Education Teaching and Learning Team, 2019)

Teaching a subject and understanding it are two different things. I think it's like someone who knows how to drive a car and a mechanic. The driver is the teacher; they understand the key concepts of how a car works and use these things on a daily basis to get from A to B. The subject lead within a primary school is the mechanic, checking in for an MOT every now and then and ready to help in an emergency. They know the 'nuts and bolts' of the subject and how to make it all work in sequence. We'd call that a curriculum within schools. The key thing for an early career teacher to know is that they have to understand these key concepts in order to be a safe driver or effective teacher. There is no need to complicate things; just get the basics consistently right and respect the road (or the subject). The overarching principle I'm digging at is that you don't need to know everything about everything, but you do need to know what you should focus on. This work *should* be done by your school's curriculum. It *should* unpick for you which overarching concepts are most important for children to understand in order to learn, enjoy and engage with a subject.

When teaching any curriculum subject, whether it be a foundation subject or any other, there are overarching concepts for you to consider and ensure are being made explicit to your class of learners. The concept of multiplication is fundamental to being a competent mathematician. Punctuation and an understanding of verbs, nouns, adverbs etc are all vital to understand for any child wanting to construct effective sentences and develop the ability to write fluently. Most teachers tend to be aware of these for the core subjects but perhaps are not so confident when it comes to the foundation subjects. Just as a child who doesn't know the difference between a noun and a verb by Year 5 is highly likely to struggle in English, the same can be said for a child who doesn't understand democracy in history or migration in geography. The fact is, whatever topic you are teaching within these subjects, it is highly likely that these key concepts are going to be underpinning the subject. This is why the distinction between 'topic' and 'subject' are so important. Remember Mary Myatt's point from earlier in the book?

> If I understand the big idea behind something, it means new information is more likely to stick.
>
> (Myatt, 2020)

This is why an understanding of the key concepts of a subject are so important. If a child understands the concept of power in history, they can apply that knowledge to any 'topic' you teach. Romans, Tudors, Nazi Germany and most other significant moments in history revolve around the battle for power. If children can understand this key concept, they will be able to apply it to any point in history and, as Myatt says, information about each of these topics is far more likely to stick.

To put it into really simple terms: when you hire a car, there will be nuances and individual requirements for the hire car compared to the one you usually drive. The dials may be somewhere different, the biting point of the accelerator is far higher or there is an automatic rather than a manual gear box. Although it will feel uncomfortable for a while, your understanding of the key concepts of how a car works will allow you to very quickly adjust and become familiar with the new car.

This is the same process for children when they are tackling new topics at school. Concepts can make the process of understanding new information far, far easier.

This is backed up by the theory and research that underpins many schools' approaches to curriculum design. Hattie (2012) notes that prior knowledge is one of the most influential factors in learning. While children may possess the appropriate prior knowledge, they may not make connections between this and the new content, hence the importance of prompting children to recall previous learning before the presentation of new knowledge.

You increase the likelihood that your students will be able to recall and use what you teach by helping them engage their prior knowledge and connect new information to their prior understanding. New learning is constructed on prior knowledge. The more you understand what students already think, and the more you help them engage their prior understanding, the more likely they are to learn well. With this fresh in your mind, you can see why schools will try to ensure their curriculum is well sequenced and coherent in its design across age phases. Although it is inevitable that children will be learning different topics across their time in primary school, if you can ensure the same concepts are being revisited through the lens of each of those topics, you will have lessons that build on prior knowledge and allow new bits of information to stick.

# So what?

Across two chapters you have looked at the importance of identifying and using key concepts to underpin your foundation subject teaching. How you teach these key concepts is a vital component to ensuring the knowledge is not just on the lesson plan but actively happening during learning time. In order for that to happen, you need to make sure you are explicitly teaching your children what these concepts are. You need to be enthusiastic about engaging in debates and discussions with your classes to really understand what is meant by power in history, migration in geography or beliefs in RE. It's vital that during these discussions, you are not defining what is right and wrong. Guiding the children to understand what these terms mean is essential but questions, misinterpretations, reinterpretations and open discussion are what will allow your classes to really 'get under the skin' of these wide-ranging concepts.

It's important at this point to acknowledge that *there must be one agreed set of key concepts for each school subject.* People and groups have different views on this. Subjects are constantly growing and changing, so it is unlikely there could ever be just one agreed set of key concepts for all learning situations. However, it is often useful in a particular context (for example, an examination specification) to present a set of key concepts, as these can then be used to help plan the curriculum. This is where using the national curriculum can be a useful starting point for teachers and schools.

As with anything worth doing, it won't come easy. You need to take on board some of the suggestions from earlier in the book. Good planning will be essential if you are to ensure these concepts are being revisited often enough for them to be established in the children's minds. You will need to ensure that you have given enough learning time over to the discussions and debates that will underpin some of this crucial work and, most importantly, you will need to be able to identify and prioritise these concepts during your planning. This is the part where your skill as a teacher kicks in. Taking a scheme of work and delivering it to a group of children is tough but doable. The best teachers are the ones who take that platform and enrich it with their own understanding of the subject, their own passions and enthusiasm. Are you going to focus solely on the ability of the miniature avatar on Scratch to dance across the screen, or will you reward the children who show creativity in giving something a go and pushing the boundaries of whatever task they have been given? A key concept within computing is the willingness to use technology to try new things, break barriers and make sure you're getting the most out of whichever tech you are using. When the children settle down to have a conversation in Spanish, is it all about their ability to speak fluently? Or will you ensure the children are able to have discussions about the origin of language and the similarities between languages? The truth is you make the weather. Ultimately, whatever happens in your classroom is unequivocally down to you and your choices. It's my favourite thing about being a teacher: the opportunity to create something new and exciting, every single day. The scary part of that is that it is entirely down to you. You can embrace that challenge by widening your children's minds with rich discussion and learning around the key concepts that drive not only foundation subjects, but society and life as a whole.

## Case study ◀◀◀

### Keeping things simple

*Jennifer Lagos – Key Stage 1 teacher*

*I continue to find teaching really hard. There are so many elements to a successful lesson and no matter how many years I am in the classroom, I continue to find it tough. One of the many things I have learnt throughout the years is that I can make it more complicated or simpler for myself and the children. When looking at the national curriculum, I felt lost. It seemed like there were so many things for me to cover, it* was hard to prioritise and know what to teach first. My school curriculum would often tell me which topic to teach but very little detail beyond that. I would spend my PPA trying to squeeze as much information and content into my lesson plans as possible, through fear of not having covered what I needed to. Unfortunately, the outcome of that meant I would end up teaching lessons without a clear outcome and with muddled thinking for both me and the children. One way of keeping things as simple as possible is to focus on what key concepts underpin a subject.

There is only so much knowledge that children can cling onto, especially if it is new information without context. After a few years of teaching the same year group, I started to realise that although the different topics within each subject needed to be focused on and unpicked, there were key concepts that I could revisit each time I taught a subject. When I think about it now, it's pretty obvious because it's how I teach the core subjects. Each year, the children revisit the same mathematical concepts, just at a different level and with different contexts. Year 1 might be adding together sweets, focusing on one-digit numbers, but Year 6 are still focusing on addition, it's just not with sweets and now involves far more than one digit! Why wouldn't music or history be exactly the same? Year 1 looking at rhythm in a very simplistic and basic way before Year 6 look at rhythm in far more depth and with higher expectation of outcome. The challenge for me has been identifying what those key concepts for each subject are and trying to make sure I include them in all of my planning and teaching.

## Reflective task ◀◀◀

1.  What are the implications for you as an early career teacher?

2.  What can you learn from this to further your development?

3.  What one thing will you do differently as a consequence of this case study?

# Now what? ◀ ◀ ◀

## Practical task for tomorrow ◀◀◀

Access the English national curriculum website (www.gov.uk/government/publications/national-curriculum-in-england-primary-curriculum) to find the attainment targets from each curriculum subject across Key Stages 1 and 2.

*   Spend some time considering each target and try to identify what you think would be a 'big idea' or key concept to look at in depth with the children in your class.

Remember, concepts are key themes for each subject that are likely to be revisited no matter what topic you are covering. Table 4.1 is an example of how you can do this, using the art and design primary national curriculum document, perfectly illustrating how a school can ensure all teachers are focusing on the same concepts across year groups. In the following text, the key concepts within the national curriculum text are highlighted, while Table 4.1 exemplifies each concept and how they might look in practice. The concepts are focused on the Key Stage 1 curriculum.

## Art and design subject content Key Stage 1

Pupils should be taught:

» to use a range of materials creatively to design and make products;

» to use drawing, painting and sculpture to develop and share their ideas, experiences and imagination;

» to develop a wide range of art and design techniques in using colour, pattern, texture, line, shape, form and space;

» about the work of a range of artists, craft makers and designers, describing the differences and similarities between different practices and disciplines, and making links to their own work.

## Art and design subject content Key Stage 2

Pupils should be taught to develop their techniques, including their control and their use of materials, with creativity, experimentation and an increasing awareness of different kinds of art, craft and design.

Pupils should be taught:

» to create sketch books to record their observations and use them to review and revisit ideas;

» to improve their mastery of art and design techniques, including drawing, painting and sculpture with a range of materials (for example, pencil, charcoal, paint, clay);

» about great artists, architects and designers in history.

**Table 4.1 St Mary's Catholic Academy**

| Subject | Concept from national curriculum | Exemplification |
|---|---|---|
| Art and design | Line | Short or continuous marks made using a variety of tools. Lines can define the edge of a contour or shape and can be straight, curved, broken or continuous, thick or thin. Lines can be used to represent texture and form by hatching and cross hatching. |
| | Shape | Shape is created by enclosing a space using an outline. The shape of an object or geometric pattern and the shape between objects. |
| | Form | Description of 3D shape; form has volume and occupies space. It can be regular, eg a cube or sphere, or irregular, eg a stone, shell or a fir cone. |
| | Space | The unlimited three-dimensional expanse in which all objects are located. The distance between two points. The illusion of space can be created through the use of colour, tone, linear perspective and scale. |
| | Colour | We are surrounded by colour – take a look! There are three primary colours: red, blue and yellow. They can be used to mix secondary colours: green, purple and orange. |
| | Tone | Differences in light and dark, tint or shade of colour to show effect of light on colour and form. Lighter tones or tints can be made by adding black to a colour. |
| | Texture | Describes how something feels, the surface quality of an object. Rough, smooth, hard, soft, prickly, spiky, furry. |

- The final concept that can be taken from the art and design national curriculum is 'pattern'. Use Table 4.1 as a model to try and create some exemplification ideas for the concept of pattern.

| Subject | Concept from national curriculum | Exemplification |
|---|---|---|
| Art and design | Pattern | |

It may well be the case that your school does not have a document similar to this one for each or any of your subjects. Nor is it your job as an early career teacher to create documents like this. However, you can spend time looking through the national curriculum and pick out key concepts for yourself to become familiar with and focus your planning on. If teachers can articulate what these key concepts are to the children in their class, revisit them through the lens of different topics and allow the children to apply their knowledge to different contexts, then deep learning will take place.

## Practical task for next week ◀◀◀

Once you have identified some of the key concepts that are outlined in the national curriculum, start to consider how you might build these into the existing planning that you have. You might want to look through and see if your planning already demonstrates some of these key concepts to save you from recreating something that already exists. Now you should be able to have a keen focus on these concepts during your teaching, which will allow the children in your class to feel confident and make progress across the curriculum. Keep in mind that returning to these concepts through the lens of different topics is vital in order for the knowledge to be embedded in long- term memory.

As an example, the concept of using rhyme for songs is a key concept for children to understand. This concept could be explored during a topic focusing on the Great Fire of London through the nursery rhyme 'London's Burning'. The same concept of rhyming could be revisited later in the year through a more obvious lens of a music topic focusing on how to identify rhyming words and creating rhyming songs. This could be linked to your new topic, whatever that might be. The key thing is that you are revisiting knowledge and skills throughout the year, in different contexts, to make sure that the learning is able to stick and be transferred into long-term memory. It is crucial that children have the chance to apply this knowledge in new contexts to deepen their learning.

## Practical task for the longer term ◀◀◀

Information needs to be linked to previous knowledge, in order for it to be easily retained and have valuable context. Having spent time looking at the key concepts that exist within the national curriculum and then how that filters down into your planning, start to look at how you can have joined-up thinking between topics across your year. What concepts can you return to again and again but through the lens of different subjects? By outlining this and prioritising it within your planning, you will allow your learners to deepen their understanding of these subject-specific concepts and they will begin to make links themselves. When this starts to happen, children begin to build passion and enjoyment within a subject, to the point that they will hopefully become lifelong learners far beyond their time in your classroom.

Daniel Willingham's description of how we come to remember information is a good example of this principle in action.

> *Whatever you think about, that's what you remember.* Memory is the residue of thought. *Once stated, this conclusion seems impossibly obvious. Indeed, it's a very sensible way to set up a memory system. Given that you can't store everything away, how should you pick what to store and what to drop? Your brain lays its bets this way: If you don't think about something very much, then you probably won't want to think about it again, so it need not be stored.*
>
> (Willingham, 2010, p 18)

The implication for teachers is that if a key concept is only visited once or twice, it is highly unlikely that the children will remember this information. They may have covered it and it may have been taught to them but, critically, they may not have remembered it. By planning ahead and identifying those key concepts, holding them clearly in your mind and therefore your planning, you have a very good chance of making a significant impact on the children in your class.

# What next?

## Further reading

Bellingham-Young, D (2015) Developing a Basic Principles Model to Inform Threshold Concepts of Public Health. *Journal of Health and Social Care Improvement.* [online] Available at: https://wlv.openrepository.com/bitstream/handle/2436/611822/Denise-Bellingham-Young-April-2015_1.pdf (accessed 12 December 2022).

Garwal, P K, Finley, J R, Rose, N S and Roediger, H L (2017) Benefits from Retrieval Practice Are Greater for Students with Lower Working Memory Capacity. *Memory*, 25(6): 764–71.

Kirschner, P, Sweller, J, Kirschner, F and Zambrano, J (2018) From Cognitive Load Theory to Collaborative Cognitive Load Theory. *International Journal of Computer-Supported Collaborative Learning*, 13: 213–33.

Ofsted (2021) Curriculum Research Reviews. [online] Available at: www.gov.uk/government/collections/curriculum-research-reviews (accessed 12 December 2022).

Sweller, J (2016) Working Memory, Long-term Memory, and Instructional Design. *Journal of Applied Research in Memory and Cognition*, 5(4): 360–7.

# References

International Education Teaching and Learning Team (2019) Get Started with Key Concepts. [online] Available at: https://cambridge-community.org.uk/professional-development/gswkey/index.html (accessed 10 February 2023).

Hattie, J (2012) *Visible Learning for Teachers*. Oxford: Routledge.

Murphy, G (2002) *The Big Book of Concepts*. Cambridge, MA: MIT Press.

Myatt, M (2020) Concepts [online]. Available at: www.marymyatt.com/blog/concepts (accessed 12 December 2022).

St Mary's Catholic Academy (2022) Key Concepts in Art. [online] Available at: www.stmarysstoke.co.uk/key-concepts-in-art (accessed 12 December 2022).

Willingham, D T (2010) The Myth of Learning Styles. *Change: The Magazine of Higher Learning*, 42(5): 32–5.

Young, M, Lambert, D, Roberts, C and Roberts, M (2014) *Knowledge and the Future School: Curriculum and Social Justice*. London: Bloomsbury Academic.

# Chapter 5   Finding time: how to plan foundation subjects

## What? (The big idea)

### Planning that supports your pupils and you

*If you don't know where you're going, you'll never get there.*

(Wiliam, 2011)

The purpose of this chapter is to not lecture you too much on how to plan a lesson. There are key principles to lesson planning that this book looks at and these are important, but the main focus will be on how to find time to plan for foundation subjects. We have already looked at how packed the primary curriculum is and if the teacher themselves does not value every subject, they simply won't be taught. Fortunately, the main thing you need when considering how to squeeze all that you can from the curriculum is creativity. Something primary school teachers have in abundance.

When considering the key principles for planning foundation subjects, it's important not to move away from the same principles used in any other subjects. Everything you will be learning about the sequencing of lessons using long, medium and short-term planning is all applicable to foundation subjects. The purpose of this book is not to teach you these key skills but to help you adapt and use them in the foundation subject space. An important principle to keep in your mind is this: foundation subjects need to be *taught* not just *covered*.

It is easy to say that you have covered the Romans, volcanoes, music composition and so on, but covering a subject is not the same as teaching it. Filling in worksheets from a popular internet resource bank is not teaching a subject. All of the research around cognitive science and the way children learn means we know that information won't be learned unless it is taught in a way that supports information being moved from short-term to long-term memory. You need to identify what you want to teach, how you plan to teach it and how the children are going to remember the information you teach. Let's use a widely recognised approach to effective teaching and learning: Rosenshine's (2012) ten key principles of instruction.

1. Daily review.

2. Present new material using small steps.

3. Ask questions.

4. Provide models.

5. Guide student practice.

6. Check for student understanding.

7. Obtain a high success rate.

8. Provide scaffolds for difficult tasks.

9. Independent practice.

10. Weekly and monthly review.

It's very likely you're already aware of these principles and using them within the classroom to support your teaching and learning process. The genius in Rosenshine's principles lies in their simplicity. You can lift them from the page and apply them to almost any subject in any key stage to support you with your planning process. Figure 5.1 illustrates that process.

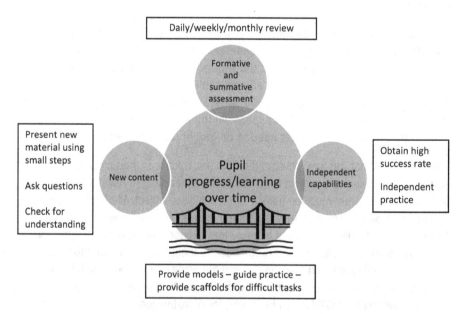

**Figure 5.1 Model for teaching new material**

The model shows how any new material from any subject can be given and taught to a class of children. The bridge demonstrates the journey from being given new and exciting information to understanding that information and being able to use it independently. Exemplifying this model might look like this. Imagine that the children are introduced to the different notes on a recorder. To begin with, they are asking questions about how to press their lips against the mouthpiece, why the thumb hole is at the back and what notes they can play. You'll start to tell them what they are required to learn during the lesson/sequences of lessons and then present them with the new material. In this case, it would be how to play a note or a song (this is the *new content* segment of the model). Once you have introduced this material, you would want to start allowing them to practise, but this will need to be heavily scaffolded. Perhaps use iPads with a video demonstrating how to play the note. You may have a carrousel with adults working in groups to support learners. There might be music books with visual demonstrations for the children to copy. Either way, you are beginning to bridge the gap between new knowledge and known knowledge. The only way that process happens is by effective teaching in the early phase of a lesson, guided and focused practice during the lesson or possibly over a sequence of lessons to allow the children to move to the final part of the model: the opportunity and ability to understand, apply and remember the learning. By the end of the sequence, the children will be able to perform a small piece of music without the scaffolding that has been in place during the learning of previous lessons.

We've used a music example, but it can be applied across all subjects. In design and technology, it might be the basic ingredients and recipe to follow to bake a cake; in geography, how lakes are formed. The subject is different each time but the process you'll follow remains largely the same.

With anything that appears to be 'one size fits all', there is a health warning. Each subject and each lesson will look and feel different. The tone of the lesson may change. Your behaviour management in PE is likely to look profoundly different to how it might look in RE or science. Despite these important differences, the key principles of how learning takes place are unlikely to change.

## Reflective task ◀◀◀

Let's consider the first step outlined in Figure 5.1, 'new content'. You already know how fundamental it is that new knowledge links back to prior knowledge in order for it to 'stick'. It's important, therefore, that your planning considers what has been taught prior to the lesson, within that **subject**. It is crucial that you do not confuse subject with topic. Remember, the topic is the vehicle through which the concepts of the subject are taught. So when you talk about introducing new content, it's important that you frame this within the idea that you will be revising key concepts within a new context. If you were looking at the concept of power in history, then when you introduce new content around Adolf Hitler and the Second World War, you need to ensure you revisit some of the key points around power and war. This allows your pupils to engage with the new content in a far more relatable way. Without the link of the concept to join up known knowledge with new knowledge, you are expecting pupils to use only their short-term memory, the part of their memory that has limited resource, to remember this new information. This will almost certainly lead to the new content being forgotten and learning being lost.

Figure 5.2 contains three questions you can prompt your pupils to consider after each sequence of learning. For Key Stage 1 classes, you may want to tweak the language but keep the underlying principle. By sharing these, you are encouraging your learners to be reflective and question their learning but you are also able to identify which key concepts have been understood and where there may be gaps in knowledge that need to be revisited through the lens of a future topic.

**Figure 5.2  Three questions to check understanding**
(Son et al, 2020)

For the purpose of the reflective task, go through these questions and replace the word 'class' in the triangle with 'book'. There is likely to be lots of new knowledge within the chapters of this book and so reflecting on which areas are making sense and which are confusing you will help you to take appropriate next steps and better understand your own development.

# So what? ◀ ◀ ◀

Remembering that covering a subject is very different to teaching it, it is important to recognise and acknowledge the reality for most primary school teachers. I am not for a minute suggesting any teacher doesn't want to teach a range of subjects. With a lack of capacity and an ever-growing list of responsibilities, it can feel as though you have no time or space to plan and teach foundation subjects. This is a legitimate concern to have and a big responsibility lies with the school to ensure there is time within the curriculum to value all subjects. This book can't help with any strategic decisions schools may be making but, assuming you are in a school where there is a desire to teach foundation subjects effectively, then let's look at some ideas for best practice.

The process for planning within your school is very likely to look as depicted in Figure 5.3.

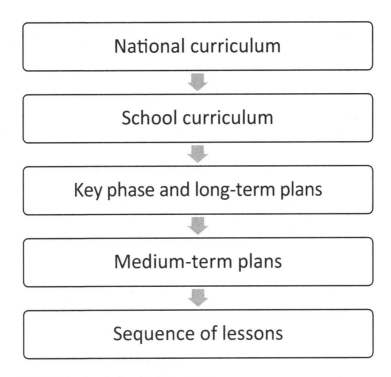

**Figure 5.3  Wider school planning process**

Typically, each school will use the national curriculum to inform their own school curriculum choices. Once that process has been completed, usually by the school senior leadership team, it will then be used to create some longer-term plans and specific topics for each year group to cover (for example, the Tudors in Year 2; the Second World War in Year 5). This is likely to be managed by a subject lead for your school. Once that has been created, it's then down to the teacher of each year group to create some engaging lessons around the topics they have been given for each subject. This should mean that a large part of your job has been done for you, by your fabulous colleagues in school. The teacher's job is to add the icing and cherry: the creative and fun bit of planning a sequence of lessons.

One of my favourite phrases when it comes to professional work is that *'there is no need to reinvent the wheel'*. If something high quality already exists, then there is definitely no need to create work that does not need doing – you're busy enough already. If you have some excellent planning for each foundation subject, you are one of the lucky ones and you should enjoy it for all it is worth. Ensure the planning meets the current level of understanding of the children in your class and inspires the next generation of composers, geologists, actors, etc.

If you don't have that planning in place, then it falls upon your shoulders to create it. Continue reading this book (well, you've made it this far) and engage with the final section, which highlights the very best places to find support and information for each foundation subject. You may find something that has already been created to support you on your journey to planning and teaching amazing foundation subject lessons.

The best piece of advice when it comes to planning engaging lessons is this: if you find it interesting, there's a good chance the children will do too. You will also find the process of planning your sequence of lessons far more enjoyable. The old adage that *'the more you put into it, the more you get out'* is applicable in this context. The sad truth is that nobody is going to find more hours in a week for you to be able to do everything for everyone. Inevitably, there will be things that you wanted to do that you can't. Take the pressure off yourself and understand that is a reality of being a teacher, whether you want that reality or not. Returning to the first point raised at the start of this chapter: teachers who teach foundation subjects are creative; not only with their planning but also with their time. This book can't tell you how to split your time during PPA or once the children have gone home. The hope is that it can emphasise how grateful so many children in your class will be if you value the subjects they have a natural affection for. A natural skill or talent. A passion. Teachers achieve more in a week than most other professions aim for in a month; it's the environment we know and planning engaging foundation subject lessons is a fundamental part of ensuring that, despite these pressures, we are able to enjoy a varied and challenging role in school.

## Case study ◀◀◀

### Efficiency over box ticking

*Amari Jelani – Key Stage 2 teacher*

*As a beginner teacher, planning and marking were the two biggest drains of my time. I could get to the end of a PPA session and feel as though I'd achieved nothing despite having spent hours trying to create engaging lessons for my class to learn from. When it came to core subjects, my school had a plethora of* planning for each year group to build from but due to a recent Ofsted inspection, all of the foundation subject planning was being recreated. As a newly qualified teacher, this was an incredibly intimidating prospect. It was taking me twice as long as my peers to plan effectively and now I had an entire curriculum to create... from scratch! At the time, I was not grateful for the situation I found myself in but as my career has gone on, I realised how fortunate I was. I had no other option but to find a way of ensuring that I was efficient with my planning. Had I not found a way, there would have been no planning. The old adage goes 'nothing worth having comes easy' and foundation subjects fit into this well in my opinion. It can sometimes feel as though we don't have time to prioritise all subjects across the curriculum but we must fight against that feeling. Why? Not only will your children benefit hugely from the opportunity to engage and excel in a variety of different subjects but you will also find variety and excitement within your day. My headteacher used to talk about teaching a subject with intent. It's stuck with me to this day. If you are simply 'covering' a subject for the sake of saying 'we did it' then why bother? You need to be really clear in your mind about why you are teaching this subject and what it is you want children to learn. If you can ensure you keep a driven intent to your planning, then a lot of the confusion is stripped away and it becomes far easier to be creative and enjoy the process. If you are staring at a blank planning document, looking at the minutes tick away before the children come back from lunch and your PPA ends, prompt yourself to think about what is your intent in this lesson? What do you really want the children to learn during the 45 minutes you have for this subject? We have far more freedom as teachers than we can sometimes think. You will have a school curriculum for each subject that will loosely tell you what to teach. You then have the power to zoom in and create a sequence of lessons that your class will learn from. This is the fun bit of our job. The moment that you can take a topic and dissect it until you find all the best juicy bits to devour with your class. That can feel overwhelming when there is so much to cover, but if you can keep intent at the forefront of your mind, it's amazing how quickly your myriad of options start to narrow down to a few shining nuggets of content.

## Reflective task ◀◀◀

1. What are the implications for you as an early career teacher?

2. What can you learn from this to further your development?

3. What one thing will you do differently as a consequence of this case study?

Everything we have looked at during this chapter will be heavily influenced by the existing planning and policies within your school. The first thing you'll need to do is refer to these documents and ensure you understand what expectations your school has and the quality of the planning that already exists. Remember – there is no point reinventing the wheel if it isn't necessary. Once you have familiarised yourself with your school's approach, start to consider how you are going to impact on pupil progress. What does success look like within the context of your school? Remember that the children in your class will only be successful if you are able to articulate to them what success looks like.

# Now what?

## Practical task for tomorrow

Spend some time reflecting on your own hobbies and consider what influenced these hobbies when you were younger. Was it a parent, family member or friend who first introduced you to your hobby? Perhaps your enjoyment started when you were at school, influenced by a teacher who was passionate about a subject? Try to use the passion you have for whatever hobby you have identified as a template for what you are trying to achieve within the children you teach. Tap into what makes it enjoyable for you and try to create the same feeling within your learners.

## Practical task for next week

Speak to your senior leadership team and ask if you can use your early career teacher PPA time to focus solely on foundation subject planning. One of the challenges as an early career teacher is that it can feel as though there are so many things to focus on and improve that prioritising can become difficult. By allowing yourself some time to really focus in on foundation subject planning, you will be able to buy back some time later in the term. Not only that, but you will have some high-quality lessons to deliver for the children in your class. When using this time, try to ensure you engage with the subject associations listed later in this book to get the support you'll need.

## Practical task for the longer term

As a profession, recording yourself teaching is something teachers are still learning to become comfortable with. It's perfectly understandable as nobody really likes to hear or see themselves back after doing anything, let alone teaching. However, the benefits of doing so should far outweigh your natural reluctance. Instructional coaching models are becoming embedded within schools; indeed, you will likely be following such a model during your early career teacher years. The hope is that this creates a generation of teachers who feel it is totally normal to record and watch back their teaching.

The benefit for the purposes of this book is that it will allow you to watch back a foundation subject lesson and compare it against one of your core subject lessons. What, if any, are the differences? Not just for you but the children. Is there a difference in engagement with either lesson? Why? Your own perception of how a lesson went can be very hard to get right as you are thinking about a million-and-one things at the front of the class. It's impossible to remember it all. By periodically recording yourself teach and watching it back, you are able to truly analyse your practice and then make the positive changes you want to see in your teaching for the benefit of the learners in your class.

# What next? ◀ ◀ ◀

## Further reading

Coe, R, Aloisi, C, Higgins, S and Major, L E (2014) *What Makes Great Teaching? Review of the Underpinning Research*. Durham University. [online] Available at: http://bit.ly/2OvmvKO (accessed 12 December 2022).

Didau, D and Rose, N (2016) *What Every Teacher Needs to Know About Psychology*. Woodbridge: John Catt Educational Limited.

Dunlosky, J, Rawson, K A, Marsh, E J, Nathan, M and Willingham, D T (2013) Improving Students' Learning with Effective Learning Techniques: Promising Directions from Cognitive and Educational Psychology. *Psychological Science in the Public Interest*, 14(1): 4–58.

Eaude, T and Catling, S (2020) The Role of Humanities in a Broad and Balanced Curriculum. [online] Available at: https://my.chartered.college/impact_article/the-role-of-the-humanities-in-a-balanced-and-broadly-based-primary-curriculum (accessed 12 December 2022).

Mounstevens, E and Astolfi, C (2020) The Spiral Curriculum Approach. [online] Available at: https://my.chartered.college/impact_article/the-spiral-curriculum-approach (accessed 12 December 2022).

Myatt, M and Tomsett, J (2021) *Huh: Curriculum Conversations Between Subject and Senior Leaders*. Woodbridge: John Catt Education Ltd.

# References

Nussbaum, M (2010) *Not for Profit: Why Democracy Needs the Humanities*. Princeton, NJ: Princeton University Press.

Rosenshine, B (2012) Principles of Instruction: Research-based Strategies That All Teachers Should Know. *American Educator*. [online] Available at: www.aft.org/sites/default/files/Rosenshine.pdf (accessed 12 December 2022).

Son, K, Brittingham Furlonge, N and Agarwal, P (2020) *Metacognition: How to Improve Student's Reflections on Learning*. Klingenstein Center. [online] Available at: http://pdf.retrievalpractice.org/MetacognitionGuide.pdf (accessed 12 December 2022).

Wiliam, D (2011) *Embedded Formative Assessment*. Bloomington, IN: Solution Tree Press.

# Chapter 6    Explicitly making links: cross-curricular approaches

## What? (The big idea)

### Understanding the difference between subject and topic

*The teaching of discrete aspects of subject knowledge and their application in cross-curricular contexts can be achieved in the same week. Through a school year, it is possible to apply new learning in each curriculum subject in a cross-curricular context.*

(Barnes, 2022)

A few years ago, a cross-curricular approach to teaching foundation subjects was seen as the 'silver bullet' for schools and teachers trying to teach a packed curriculum. There are definite benefits to using a cross-curricular approach, but it is important you don't lose the essence of individual subjects. This chapter uses the national curriculum as the starting point and then looks at what lesson planning might look like. Before it dives into the practicalities of cross-curricular approaches, let's consider what is meant by a cross-curricular approach.

Barnes would argue that you can't expect children to thrive in a modern world without the ability to understand a subject from a variety of viewpoints and angles. This builds on Dewey's belief that children need to take ownership of their learning through investigation and making links to prior learning. A cross-curricular approach to teaching and learning affords you this opportunity. It makes sense that if you are studying volcanoes in geography, you could use moments in history to give context to some of the issues children will be learning about. Pompeii would be a great example of how you can weave history into some deep learning about volcanoes. The likelihood is that you will contextualise a very complex subject, such as volcanoes, for the children in your class. Your typical child growing up in the UK will most likely never have seen a volcano or understand much about them. By referring to a moment in history to give a concrete example of what can happen when a volcano erupts, you are giving them a maypole to wrap the rest of their new knowledge around. The tricky part with cross-curricular learning is ensuring that you are not confusing children with multiple desired outcomes. In the example of Pompeii, what will your learning outcome be? To understand the impact Mount Vesuvius had on the landscape of Pompeii? If that was your learning outcome, then your children are learning about geography. You might reference the historical context of Mount Vesuvius erupting and encasing an entire town in ash and soot, but you'll be focusing on the geographical principles of how that happened. What material is released when a volcano erupts? How did that material encase the town? What is the technical language linked to a volcano erupting? The danger when teaching with a cross-curricular approach is that the learning can become lost. We cover a lot of information, most of it engaging and useful, but the understanding of what success looks like is lost and this can be confusing for children.

Any fact can be found through technology – try looking up 'grooming for dogs'. You don't need a teacher to learn facts, but you do need a teacher to develop the skills to use those facts. In science you learn about the lungs and breathing. However, you also learn and apply this knowledge in PE/personal development, health and physical education, drama and music. The impact of air quality is studied in geography. Furthermore, there are implications for mathematics in measurement and statistical analysis, and English supports the skills to communicate the learning clearly and succinctly.

As the adult, a teacher should be able to see the links between subjects in any task they undertake. Make it explicit. If you are teaching lighting in a drama classroom, reference the planning needed (mathematics), the lens focus (science), the ground plan required (geography), the health and safety (personal development and health), the need to know the purpose of the lighting to further the performance (English), the positioning of performers (dance and PE), the link to other performance aspects (music), the significance and meaning of colour (visual art and RE) (Roy et al, 2015). Make these links explicit to the students.

The key when using a cross-curricular approach is to make sure the subject is not confused with the topic. A topic can be taught across a whole range of subjects, and this is often incredibly powerful and impacts hugely on children's progress. Creating a piece of music, a design and technology project, some incredible artwork and fantastic diary writing in history – all linked to the Second World War – builds on a lot of the principles that have been focused on in this book. It provides relatable information and learning that children can understand and then apply to a different context. This deepens learning and allows joined-up thinking throughout a sequence of lessons. What you don't want to lose is the distinct learning and skills that are being taught in each of those subjects. Although they are all linked to a moment in history, they are not all history lessons. You might be working on different types of brush strokes in art and will have a specific learning outcome for that lesson. Music will have been focusing on the ability to compose a piece of music, while planning and testing a prototype will have been the focus in design and technology. None of these learning outcomes have anything to do with the Second World War; it is merely the vehicle for children to use to support their learning. All too often cross-curricular learning is seen as a way of 'ticking boxes' and an easy way of ensuring curriculum coverage. The learning is watered down, and the subject-specific learning outcomes are lost.

When there is a clear distinction between the topic being covered and the distinct subjects that are using that topic to support children's learning, that's when a cross-curricular approach becomes highly powerful and can have a profound impact on both pupil outcomes and the well-being of a teacher and their often-overcrowded timetable. A cross-curricular approach allows the teacher to neatly package and wrap together a wide range of subjects into a neat topic that ensures knowledge is to be applied and understood in a variety of contexts. This deepens learning and allows the child to demonstrate their understanding across a range of different subjects. The key, and I won't apologise for labouring this point, is to not confuse the subject and the topic. They are two distinct and very different things. If you manage to keep that distinction live in your head when planning cross-curricular lessons, you will be able to create a learning environment that allows links to be made across your entire timetable, as well as offering children the chance to demonstrate their new knowledge in a variety of creative and engaging ways.

# So what?

So, it has been established that taking a cross-curricular approach, assuming that it is done in the right way, can be of huge benefit to the children in your class. Does that mean you should be looking to teach each topic with a cross-curricular approach? Well, a lot of that will depend on the policy and subject leadership within your school. As you have seen, your school's approach is fundamental to being able to teach foundation subjects effectively. However, if your school plans and delivers foundation subjects, it's very likely that you will be using a topic each term/half-term to support learning across a range of subjects. You mustn't forget the autonomy you have within your classroom. Familiarise yourself with whichever topic you are scheduled to cover, identify those areas that you think the children in your class will find particularly enlightening or engaging and then start to build learning objectives for each subject. A quick reminder here that very little of the national curriculum for foundation subjects is statutory. There are suggested topics to cover but that doesn't mean a school has to use these. Even within topics, there are subtopics. Which part of the Romans might you want to focus on? There are literally hundreds of fascinating periods of history within the Romans' dominance of Europe. One of the undeniable joys of being a teacher is the ability to pour through these periods and pick out the moments and figures that you think the children in your class will be inspired by. Once you've done that, plan some engaging and, dare I say it, fun lessons.

# Now what? ◀◀◀

It's useful to have concrete examples to hang new learning on. The evidence suggests that is how you should teach children, so why is it any different for adults? With that in mind, Table 6.1 is an example of what cross-curricular planning can look like. I'm not going to bore you with individual lesson plans but rather provide more of an overview of how a topic can be woven into the seams of different subjects. I hope this example will be a support in helping to understand what is meant. (A reminder that prior to this planning exercise, I will have familiarised myself with what other year groups are covering, as well as speaking to my subject leads to ensure that I have coverage of the key learning outcomes for my year group.)

**Table 6.1 Topic through subjects**

| Topic: Key Stage 2 Space | |
|---|---|
| **Subject** | **Potential learning outcome** |
| History | Explore key historical events from space exploration. |
| Art and design | Paint a space-themed picture, using Van Gogh's *Starry Night* as inspiration. |
| Geography | Observe the human and physical features of planets in our solar system to determine if we could live on another planet. |
| Music | Creatively respond to a piece of music – 'The Planets' – and create a soundscape. |
| Computing | Use search technologies effectively to establish facts about how the universe was established. |
| Design and technology | Design and create a shooting star that uses at least one mechanical system, eg pulley, gears, etc. |
| Physical education | Using our piece of music, 'The Planets', devise and perform a dance using a range of movement patterns. |
| Religious education | Compare the Christian creation story with the Big Bang theory. |
| Languages | Create a 30-second presentation, to be spoken in the language being covered within school. |

To be clear, you are highly unlikely to have a document that looks like Table 6.1 in school but it is helpful to articulate the points being made in this chapter. I'm hoping you can see the clear distinction between the topic of space and the subjects themselves. Although each learning objective is linked to the topic, they are also specifically focusing on skills that are subject specific. Skills such as painting, dancing and designing are all very subject specific and key concepts for children to learn. We are using the exciting and engaging vehicle of space to teach these key concepts. An approach similar to this, with an awareness of the importance of distinct subject-focused learning objectives, is the key to success when using a cross-curricular approach.

## Case study ◀◀◀

### Keeping subjects distinct

*Kalani Zhang – Key Stage 2 teacher*

*When I first started teaching, taking a 'cross-curricular' approach was seen as the perfect solution to the congested and busy primary curriculum. Schools were struggling to fit every subject into a busy timetable and so teaching subjects in one go seemed like a fantastic idea. Time saved, subjects covered and children get a rich diet of learning. In principle, this approach made sense. There are undeniable links between subjects, some of which are really useful to make explicit. Timetables are busy and squeezing two lessons into one made space that would otherwise not be there. However, one of the main downsides of this approach was that when I taught these subjects, it would be hard to distinguish what I was teaching. A geography lesson that felt more like history was a lot of fun for me and the kids but clarity was often lost around what the learning was. Each subject has its own distinct learning points and when the children are not clear on what success looks like, it can feel overwhelming. Each subject deserves its own place within our curriculum.*

*That's not to say there aren't opportunities to create lessons that are linked to other subjects. Of course, it is clear that certain elements of the RE curriculum will share common themes and issues with a subject like history. The issue was often that I wouldn't plan a clear-enough learning objective to tie it to either subject. When it is not clear what success looks like, it is very hard to teach effectively and even harder to learn. When I teach lessons that take inspiration from one subject and another, I have learnt to ensure that my learning objective is clearly aligned to the subject that is listed on the timetable. That way the learners know what is expected of them and I am able to plan activities and content that will ensure progress across the curriculum in an assessable way.*

## Reflective task

1. What are the implications for you as an early career teacher?

2. What can you learn from this to further your development?

3. What one thing will you do differently as a consequence of this case study?

# Now what?

## Practical task for tomorrow

If you are considering the possibility of using a cross-curricular approach, then you will want to ensure you are finding subjects that share areas of common ground. Look at your topic for the term and start to create a small table where you can link together subjects that will complement each other when teaching. Remember that it is key that the children in your class understand the difference between a topic and a subject so keeping this at the front of your mind during planning will be crucial.

## Practical task for next week

Look at the curriculum your school has created for foundation subjects. This is likely to be highly detailed and list a range of desired outcomes for each year group. Look through and start to highlight logical links between subjects. This includes areas that you can outline to the children in your class to allow them to understand the relationship between different subjects and therefore deepen their understanding. There is an opportunity for you to work with some experienced colleagues and find out from them how they link together subjects for the benefit of their pupils. There can be a desire to reinvent the wheel when you are at the start of your career, almost as if it is cheating to use the stuff that is already out there. A fresh new surgeon doesn't feel the need to find a new way to fix a broken leg; they watch and learn from their more experienced colleagues and then replicate all the techniques and strategies that were successful. Teaching is no different in this sense. Learn what already works and replicate it the best you can in the first instance. As you grow and become the teacher you are meant to be, you will inevitably start to make changes to your own practice. There is no need to rush or feel the need to create work that doesn't need to exist.

## Practical task for the longer term ◀◀◀

This is a tough ask and will require some planning and commitment but is a rich exercise if you're able to do it. Use one of your PPA sessions during your early career teacher years to visit a secondary school and work alongside some foundation subject teachers. Speak to them about the key concepts of their subject. Observe some lessons and see what the children are expected to know when they get to Year 7. Ask the teacher how they would link their subject to another if they were to be asked to work in a cross-curricular way. Secondary teachers are immersed in one subject in a very different way to primary school teachers. The knowledge they can give you will be invaluable on your journey to understanding the key concepts that make up each foundation subject. By observing a lesson, you will also be able to see what the expectation is of the children you are teaching when they reach secondary school. It's very hard to know what to focus on if you don't know what the end goal is and although the national curriculum gives you an end point for Key Stage 2, it's important you're as aware as possible of what comes further down the line. All in all, if you are hoping to work with a cross-curricular model, the more aware you can be of each subject's distinct areas of knowledge, the easier you will find it to make links between them.

# What next? ◀ ◀ ◀

## Further reading

Barnes, J (2015) *Cross-Curricular Learning 3–14*. London: Sage.

Eaude, T and Catling, S (2020) The Role of Humanities in a Broad and Balanced Curriculum. [online] Available at: https://my.chartered.college/impact_article/the-role-of-the-humanities-in-a-balanced-and-broadly-based-primary-curriculum (accessed 12 December 2022).

Fordham, M (2014) Making History Stick Part 2: Switching the Scale Between Overview and Depth. [online] Available at: https://clioetcetera.com/2014/08/06/making-history-stick-part-2-switching-the-scale-between-overview-and-depth (accessed 12 December 2022).

Myatt, M and Tomsett, J (2021) *Huh: Curriculum Conversations Between Subject and Senior Leaders*. Woodbridge: John Catt Education Ltd.

# References

Barnes, J (2022) Across the Curriculum. [online] Available at: https://osiriseducational.
co.uk/staffroom/article/across-the-curriculum (accessed 12 December 2022).

Roy, D, Baker, W and Hamilton, A (2015) *Teaching the Arts: Early Childhood and Primary Education*. Cambridge: Cambridge University Press.

# Chapter 7   Less but better

## What? (The big idea) ◀ ◀ ◀

### Essentialism within the classroom

*Essentialism is not about how to get more things done; it's about how to get the right things done.*

(McKeown, 2021, p 9)

The penultimate chapter of this book is possibly the most important. Think of it as a reward for having read through the first six chapters. This book has unpicked, in great detail, some of the strategies and approaches you are going to need to take in order to teach foundation subjects effectively. Lots of this has been linked to pedagogical approaches, planning, assessment and so on. In your final journey, you are going to zoom out a little bit and consider your overall approach to foundation subjects; an approach that will not only mean you get the best out of yourself but also the best out of the children in your class. Most importantly, it is an approach that will give you the longevity and energy to teach effectively year after year. Let me start by getting you to reflect on some questions.

>> Have you ever found yourself stretched too thin at work?

>> Have you ever felt both overworked and underutilised?

>> Do you ever feel busy but not productive?

>> Do you ever feel like you're constantly in motion but never getting anywhere?

I read a book recently that spoke about an approach to life called *essentialism*, written by Greg McKeown in 2021. Mary Myatt references this book within some of her own work and at the start of his first chapter, McKeown challenges you with these questions. The premise of his book is that people try to cram every opportunity into their lives, thinking it will make them happy. By ensuring that they don't miss out on anything that might be presented to them, they somehow ensure that they truly do 'have it all'. The reality is that all you are doing is watering down your enjoyment of nearly every activity you take part in. Having it all, it turns out, is a myth. Although the book was aimed at improving the reader as an individual and had nothing to do with teaching at all, I found myself drawing clear links back to my life in school and as a teacher. How often had I applied the essentialist approach to my teaching and planning? How often had I got to the end of the week and looked back thinking, '*I squeezed so much into a packed timetable and don't really feel like I achieved that much at all*'. The answer, sadly, was that I frequently felt like I was trying to 'have it all' with the curriculum choices I was making. Inevitably, it meant that nothing was ever covered in enough detail for there to be true depth of learning or joy for me or my class. So, I turned to my self-help book and started to ponder how I could apply this not only to my personal development but to my development as a teacher too. Would 'doing less but better' be the secret code to unlock the power that exists within foundation subjects? Well, my friends, the answer is an unequivocal yes.

The way the curriculum has been designed can make it look like all knowledge and information is equal. Whatever is written in the Key Stage 2 national curriculum document must be covered, each and every word. This is a common myth and it is helpful to realise that there is only a very small part of the national curriculum that is statutory. It's tempting to look at these documents and think everything is essential. But it's not. It is essential that you teach these subjects as effectively as possible, yes. But is covering every line of a document, in some sort of box-ticking exercise, essential? No. The reality of only covering what is essential within the curriculum is that you will need to make trade-offs. Too often teachers give themselves the impossible challenge of doing it all. Covering everything to the point that they actually end up covering nothing in any real detail. The motivation and philosophy behind this approach is admirable but ultimately unrealistic and doomed to fail. There is simply too much to do in a five-day week. Rather than thinking '*how can I do it all*' you should be thinking, '*what are the trade-offs here? What do I absolutely need and want to cover and what can take a back seat?*' (McKeown, 2021, p 12). Once you've worked that out, you go in big on the content you have deemed to be most important for your class/school. As a teacher you must constantly be treading the line between giving children opportunity and ensuring that you are not drowning in content for the sake of content.

Table 7.1 has been taken from Greg's book and adapted to fit a teaching model. On the left-hand side of the table sits the non-essentialist teacher. The right-hand side represents the essentialist teacher. Have a read through the two characteristics of each teacher and consider which one resonates closest with your experience of being in the classroom.

**Table 7.1 Thinks, does, gets**

|  | Non-essentialist teacher | Essentialist teacher |
|---|---|---|
| Thinks | 'I have to.' | 'I choose to.' |
|  | 'It's all important.' | 'Only a few things really matter.' |
|  | 'How can I fit it all in?' | 'What are the trade-offs?' |

|  | Non-essentialist teacher | Essentialist teacher |
| --- | --- | --- |
| Does | Reacts to what is most pressing. | Pauses to consider what really matters. |
|  | Says 'yes' to people without really thinking. | Says 'no' to everything except the essential. |
|  | Tries to force execution at the last moment. | Removes obstacles to make execution easy. |
| Gets | Takes on too much, and work suffers. | Chooses carefully in order to do great work. |
|  | Feels out of control. | Feels in control. |
|  | Is unsure of whether the right things got done. | Gets the right things done. |
|  |  | Experiences joy in the journey. |
|  | Feels overwhelmed and exhausted. |  |

Adapted from McKeown (2021)

My hope is that you are aligned perfectly with the right-hand column. However, my experience tells me that only a very small percentage of readers will find much to identify with in the right-hand column and, sadly, there will be far more familiarity with the left-hand column. Let's unpick each section together.

## Thinks

Too often in schools you believe that 'you have to' do something, without thinking about why you think that or, more importantly, questioning whether you actually *have to* do that thing. This is especially true for early career teachers who are often aware of the issues that exist within schools but very quickly fall into line with what has happened before. When you feel as though everything has the same level of importance and therefore it all needs to be done, all the time at the very best you can, no wonder it feels overwhelming. The reality is that it doesn't *have to* all be done. As qualified professionals, you are able to make a choice. Strategically and thoroughly plan out what you believe is genuinely essential. Prioritise those things and teach them in great depth. Analyse what the trade-offs are to ensure that nobody is missing anything important and then crack on and teach powerfully. An essentialist approach gives us a sense of control and control empowers people. It removes the constant feeling of not having done as much as you could have done.

To think as an essentialist teacher is not easy and it takes confidence in your own approach. You cannot only half believe in the approach. You need to recognise the benefits to you and your class and then commit to choosing what you believe is important to cover. An essentialist approach starts with changing how you think about the curriculum. Rather than seeing it as this huge space, filled with an overwhelming amount of stuff that must be delivered to children, you need to refine what exists and focus only on the things that really matter. Chapter 3 looked at how to do this through the lens of concepts within subjects. Less but better. If your mindset has this embedded in everything you do, then your PPA sessions will become more focused; your lesson planning tighter linked to deep learning; your questioning during sessions more targeted and consistent. None of that change happens unless you consciously swim against the tide and change your mindset and thinking. This is the first step towards empowering yourselves as teachers and breaking free from the shackles of believing you must fit it all in.

## Does

Once you've shifted your thinking, it is time for action. How does this new way of thinking impact on what you actually *do* in your classroom and school? This is where your discipline will start to really be tested. You will need strength and belief in your approach to be able to say 'no' to everything except the essential. The skill here is to be able to identify what is and isn't essential within the curriculum. The ability to do this as an early career teacher is incredibly difficult. You will need to lean on the experience of colleagues and your own school's curriculum content to support you. The hope is that your school will have already taken the national curriculum and highlighted key concepts and topics for you to focus on. If not, then you will need to do some legwork to look through the national curriculum and make some choices about what is essential and what is not. The beauty is that there is no wrong answer. The national curriculum, for most foundation subjects, does not tell you things you *have* to teach. It suggests things that you might want to cover and you can then pick and choose the things that really matter. Remember, you make the weather in your classroom. It's a privilege and my favourite thing about being a primary school teacher. You have the freedom to plan and teach the things you believe are important for children to understand and know.

This section is as much about what you choose *not* to do as it is about what you choose to do. You must actively say no to things in order to prioritise only the most impactful learning for your class. This will not come easily to anyone trying to master it. You may be challenged for taking a fresh approach to how you plan and teach foundation subjects and this is neither wrong nor a negative.

Professional dialogue and challenge is an essential part of how we all grow and learn as teachers. This is when clarity about the benefits of what you are doing is important. You must believe in it, commit to the approach and be prepared to back yourself. If you can stick at it for long enough, the results will speak for themselves. Do not be afraid to remove planning, activities, and so on that are already in place. Remember, the priority is the children in your class and their learning. If you believe in the principles discussed in this book, commit to changing the status quo and make difficult choices about what you are *not* going to do anymore. Very quickly, you will begin to see the impact these changes have not only on you and your happiness at work but also on the progress of the children you are teaching.

### Gets

This is the important bit but it's also the final reward for having done everything else in this chapter right. It won't come quickly but when it does, you will feel like a new person altogether. The non-essentialist teacher column in Table 7.1 is a far too familiar story for teachers across the country. They often take on too much and, as a consequence, work suffers. Teachers may feel out of control and unsure if they have focused on the right things. They may feel overwhelmed and exhausted. It is not inevitable that you end up feeling this way. You have a choice. If you use the approaches suggested throughout this book, then you can regain some of that control. You can experience joy in the journey. You'll get the right things done and know it. The essentialist teacher strives to pursue 'less but better'. This approach won't necessarily cut down your planning time. You won't go from being overworked to having loads of free time. You will still be incredibly busy and constantly challenged. What you will start to get is a deep satisfaction in your work and the ability to feel in control of your classroom. It's hard to emphasise what a difference these seemingly small outcomes can have on your own well-being and attitude towards work.

# So what?

## Don't lose joy

Instinctively, teachers know that they cannot explore every single piece of information that is given to them in the national curriculum. It's simply not possible. Discerning what is essential to explore requires you to be disciplined in how you scan and filter all the competing options that exist within the curriculum. When it comes to making these choices, it should be based on some simple metrics. You are aware of the importance of curriculum coverage, ensuring a breadth of study and that your choices are cognisant and reflective of the rich diversity the UK celebrates. However, there is one key consideration that is far too often overlooked. Fun. I remember mentioning the word *fun* during one of the earliest staff meetings of my career and it was like I had stood up and shouted expletives at the top of my lungs. Our curriculum model has been designed to focus so relentlessly on knowledge and facts that we can forget that one of the most important elements to learning or remembering something is enjoyment. True, there is deep joy and enjoyment that comes with the act of remembering something new, but it is also true that adults who don't enjoy something are unlikely to pursue it for all that long. Fun should most definitely not be the defining measure for our curriculum and teaching choices, but it needs to be a key ingredient in the mix. As the profession continues to put a central focus on the science of learning, inarguably to the benefit of every child in the classroom, there is a danger that teachers lose sight of some of the human elements of the classroom. Having fun is fundamental to most of the activities we all do throughout life. The word *school* is derived from ancient Greek and its translation is 'leisure'. Although there is a lot we can take from the science of learning, it needs to be combined with knowledge of what humans need to make them tick.

When I talk about fun, I don't just mean the children. Fun is built into the make-up of children. Activities an adult would find mundane and boring are often irresistibly exciting for a seven year-old. When you consider your curriculum choices – keeping an essentialist mindset – you should be considering what *you* would enjoy teaching. Earlier, the book spoke about the simple logic that goes with this approach. If you enjoy it, chances are the children will do too. In fact, at primary age, I guarantee you that they will enjoy it too.

Dan Rae's research tells us that to '*install a lifelong love of learning, it is imperative that students in their formative years' experience the serious benefits of fun in the classroom*' (Rae, 2000, p 28). It's important that you establish that fun doesn't need to come from a wildly planned activity or mayhem in the classroom. Fun is in learning something new and understanding it better. Fun is engaging with new content or information and being able to build on existing knowledge. Fun is partaking in a well-planned activity that involves dialogue and collaboration. In order for that to happen, teachers need to be making the right choices about which areas of the curriculum to focus on and engage children with. This is especially tough for early career teachers. The task later in the chapter is designed to try and help make that process a little easier for anyone at the beginning of their teaching journey.

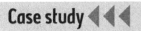

## Essentialism for you as well as the children

*Beth Scott – Previous middle leader within a primary school*

*I was someone who had always wanted to be a teacher. I left university and trained at a young age, fully expecting to be in the classroom for the foreseeable future. If someone had told me then that I would have left teaching within five years, I would have not believed it possible. I was so passionate about teaching and had worked incredibly hard to get to a point of competence that the thought I would throw that all away seemed highly unlikely. Whether I believed it or not, the truth was that after five years I did leave school and teaching. None of the reasons why I loved my job had changed but my energy, enthusiasm and commitment had been drained out of me. Not by the children or the long hours but by the feeling that I was never doing enough. By the fact that even though I worked long days, it always felt like I should be doing more. It was unsustainable and ultimately cost me the opportunity to impact on children for years to come.*

*There is a myth that teaching is tough because of the number of hours teachers work. I don't believe that to be the case. Every teacher is aware of the hours it takes to be an effective teacher; what early career teachers aren't always prepared for is the feeling of having worked relentlessly all week and feeling like they've achieved nothing. I made the mistake of thinking being busy meant I was being productive. The whole school culture was geared towards doing stuff for the sake of doing it. Rather than thinking about why we were doing something, it was just a case of doing it and then on to the next thing. I guess the main reason was because we were all too busy to stop and analyse what we were doing. The outcome of this reckless approach to working was burnout for the majority of staff and very little progress for the wider school community. The phrase 'the more you put in, the more you get out' is only true if, in the first place, you are putting the right stuff in. If you want to be a better piano player, it's true that you'll need to put in hours of practice. If that practice is misguided and focusing on the wrong things, you might have spent years of your life trying to improve but the outcome will be that you haven't made much progress. If that practice had been half the time but twice the focus on the right things, the progress would have been incomparably improved.*

*School culture wore me down to the point that I had to leave. If I had my time again, I would have ensured that the time I spent working on planning and curriculum development was more focused and driven towards clear goals and outcomes. There was nothing I could do to make teaching a less intense job; it will always be that.*

*However, I could have shifted my own focus to ensure that every hour I spent working in school was focused on the things that I knew really mattered, 'blocking out the noise' of everything else. If I'd been able to realise that, I truly believe I would have been in school for the entirety of my career.*

## Reflective task ◀◀◀

1. What are the implications for you as an early career teacher?

2. What can you learn from this to further your development?

3. What one thing will you do differently as a consequence of this case study?

# Now what? ◀ ◀ ◀

## Practical task for tomorrow ◀◀◀

Planning effective and engaging lessons is a difficult skill to master and is one that will take years of practice and experience. You can simplify the process to ensure that while you are on the journey to finding planning easier, you at least ensure you get the main parts of the process correct. Before looking at any curriculum documentation, keep these principles at the front of your mind. I call them the '3Es': enjoyment, engagement and evidence. Table 7.2 unpicks this in a little more detail.

**Table 7.2 The 3Es**

| Area of focus | Purpose of this focus |
|---|---|
| Enjoyment | When looking through your school curriculum documentation or the national curriculum, consider which elements of coverage you would find most enjoyable to look at in detail. You may have been given the Tudors as a topic to cover over six weeks. It would be impossible to cover every single element of an 118-year family monarchy so you will need make some very conscious choices about which people, moments in history, and so on that you want to focus on. By choosing the things you find most interesting as a starting point, you will find the planning process more enjoyable and far easier as you will have ownership over it. |

| Area of focus | Purpose of this focus |
|---|---|
| Engagement | Once you have identified which areas of the curriculum you are going to be sharing with the children in your class, it's time to consider how you will engage the children. This will be the 'nuts and bolts' of your lesson. You will consider how to bring the topic alive through highly effective teaching and learning strategies and high-quality questioning. Essentially, you are now beginning to plan what your teaching element of each lesson is going to look like. |
| Evidence | The final step is considering how the children will demonstrate what they have learnt during the unit of work. Will they be creating a diary entry or a podcast? Perhaps an art and design project to summarise the deep learning that has taken place? Essentially, you are considering what outcome there will be from all the rich learning that has taken place throughout your lessons on the relevant topic. Again, this process will be far more enjoyable and immeasurably easier if you have used an essentialist approach to your curriculum choices and based them around things that you think both yourself and the children will enjoy learning about. |

# Practical task for next week ◀◀◀

Consider how you might be able to adopt an essentialist approach to your wider teaching ethos. Teachers are inherently conscious people and care deeply about their jobs. This conscientious nature can be both a blessing and a curse. At its best, being conscientious means we go the extra mile and support children to be the very best they can be. At its worst, we end up trying to do too much and achieving very little in any great depth, meaning our impact is watered down to very little despite being constantly busy.

Your first step is to start a very simple journal. Not a journal of feelings and thoughts but a very practical journal that just details what you are spending your time doing. Alongside the journal, create your own system to highlight how productive each of the activities you carried out was. I use a simple green, yellow and red system. Green means very productive activity. Yellow is usually a task that I needed to do but didn't achieve much in, and red signifies a task that had minimal impact on either myself or the children and is normally time I could have used far more productively.

After two weeks, keep an eye on how many reds you are seeing pop up in your journal. How could those reds be turned into something more productive? Are they things you *have* to do? Chances are they are things you *think* you have to do and with some conscious thought, you could probably eliminate them from your working week. If you are scared to cut things out, speak to your early career teacher mentor and ask them for advice about why you are carrying these tasks out and check to see if they are things you really do need to do. Teachers frequently carry out tasks that they don't need to do through habit rather than necessity. Keeping track of what you are doing each week can ensure that you don't sleepwalk into bad habits that will eat into your time and make trying to embrace an essentialist approach impossible.

## Practical task for the longer term ◀◀◀

The focus for this task is going to be very much long-term thinking. As much as it will feel like a long way off in your early career, sooner rather than later you will be given the opportunity to lead a subject within school. There will be lots to learn when that time comes and plenty of new challenges for you to overcome. However, you can pass on the gift of essentialist thinking to the staff you will be supporting. When the opportunity comes to be an inspiring leader, most likely of a foundation subject, ensure you apply the principles spoken about throughout this book for the benefit of your colleagues. The clarity, purpose and vision you will give them by simplifying what curriculum coverage looks like and allowing a real depth of learning, focusing on key concepts across year groups, will inspire them to teach these subjects more effectively than ever before. Leadership may seem like a long way ahead in your career, and some reading this will know already that leadership is not a pathway that they'll want to pursue. However, the fact is that most teachers will be responsible for leading one area of the curriculum within the first few years of their career, and the more prepared you can be, the easier the transition will be for you.

# What next? ◀◀◀

## Further reading

Newport, C (2016) *Deep Work: Rules for Focus in a Distracted World*. New York: Grand Central Publishing.

Tomsett, J and Uttley, J (2020) *Putting Staff First: A Blueprint for Revitalising Our Schools: A Blueprint for a Revitalised Profession*. Woodbridge: John Catt Educational Ltd.

# References

McKeown, G (2021) *Essentialism: The Disciplined Pursuit of Less.* London: Virgin Books.

Myatt, M (2020) *Back on Track. Fewer Things, Greater Depth.* Woodbridge: John Catt Educational Ltd.

Rea, D (2000) *The Serious Benefits of Fun in the Classroom.* Middle School Journal, 31(4). doi:10.1080/00940771.2000.11494635.

# Chapter 8    What comes next and where to find support

## What comes next

You are coming to the end of your journey through the landscape of foundation subjects. I am unapologetic about how strongly I believe that the need to value and teach these subjects is fundamental to the development of a well-rounded and knowledgeable class of children. As has been discussed, the system often makes it hard to spend time and energy on these subjects. I hope that having read through some of the suggestions made, you feel not only enthusiastic about the idea of teaching foundation subjects effectively but empowered to do so. You have autonomy in your classroom to do the things that you care about. The things you know will make a difference in the lives of the children in your class. Throughout all my years as a teacher and working in education more widely, I have never been more confident of anything than every child deserves to be given the opportunity to learn about the things they enjoy. The things they are good at. The things that will bring them success and happiness in life. Without a wide and varied curriculum, that opportunity is taken away from your classes. You have the opportunity to prevent that from happening, and I hope this book has supported you in believing that you can do this.

This series is aimed at early career teachers and so it is likely that you will have some protected time outside of the classroom over the next few years. Time is the most precious commodity of any teacher. We very rarely have it and yet it can make such a difference to both our well-being and our ability to teach effectively. You are encouraged to use these hours as effectively as possible. You will have lots to focus on and plenty of competing priorities but foundation subjects deserve some of this time. If you can feel confident teaching across the curriculum at an early stage of your career, you will be saving yourself lots of time and effort once that extra protected time out of the classroom has gone.

As you move through your career, it is likely that you will spend less time in the classroom and more time looking at your work through the lens of the whole school, as opposed to just your class. That means it is a rare thing to be able to focus fully on the teaching and learning that is taking place hour by hour within the four walls of your classroom. During your first few years as a teacher, you have the opportunity to really impact directly on the lives of the children in your class without the distractions of leadership roles and responsibilities. Through reading this book and some of the other recommended texts and articles highlighted in previous chapters, you will feel empowered to teach the way you want to teach. Ultimately, you are accountable for the children in your class and you will be the best teacher version of yourself when you are true to who you are and what you believe in. One of the other titles in this series of books, *Mental Well-being and Self Care*, talks at length about the power of core values being met through your work. A lot of that comes from ownership of what you are doing and having autonomy in your classroom. We've peeled back the planning process and looked at how you can take the guidance given by the school curriculum and then use that as the platform from which to create a learning environment that is rich and broad. Ausubel (1968) stated that:

> if I had to reduce all of educational psychology into just one principle, I would say this 'The most important single factor influencing learning is what the learner already knows. Ascertain this and teach [them] accordingly.'

All subjects across the curriculum are complex and dense in relation to the content that *could* be covered. The key to unlocking the potential of both the subject and your learners is that you focus on the right things and concepts, at the right time and that you revisit them over and over again. There is now a keen focus on evidence-informed practice in the classroom and so much of that revolves around cognitive load theory and working memory. We know that information that is linked to things we already know is far more likely to, as Myatt (2021) puts it, stick. When foundation subjects operate as islands, and year groups are not joined up in terms of their thinking or curriculum, new knowledge is highly unlikely to make sense or be remembered. Using some of the strategies and approaches within this book will lead you to the conclusion that foundation subjects have an incredibly important place in the curriculum and, more importantly, in your classroom. The very best schools, classrooms and teachers set the children up to succeed in wider life and society. In a job market that is so diverse, it is essential that you prepare your children to be successful in whatever area they have a natural interest or talent in. Without their computing, cooking, music, geography and other lessons, they may never find that calling. Teaching is a lot of things, but essentially we are here to help young people to achieve their very best and fulfil whatever it is they are destined to go and do. What a privilege. Embrace it, live it, breathe it and be that teacher who inspires children across the whole curriculum.

The truth is that if all you rely on is the quality of your school curriculum or planning documents, you can't guarantee that children will be exposed to the high-quality, richly diverse and inspiring teaching that they deserve. The only way to guarantee that is for teachers to embrace the responsibility themselves. Whatever you prioritise within the classroom is ultimately what the children will benefit from. During your early years as a teacher, you will have competing priorities for your time. I hope you do not come away from this book feeling as though you aren't doing a good enough job if you haven't yet 'nailed' your foundation subject coverage. I was a foundation subjects lead for the majority of my time in schools and still hadn't found the perfect balance. What I did do was make sure that I gave each subject the respect, time and energy it deserved. I go back to my original point made right at the start of this book. Not all children in your class will go on to be mathematicians or authors. Plenty will become plumbers or electricians, musicians or playwriters, archaeologists or chefs. Without that initial spark in your classroom, those dreams and ambitions may never be realised. That is the privilege we have chosen to embrace as teachers. The power to find a passion within a child that, until that point, they didn't know existed.

## Where to find support

The first place to highlight is your school. It sounds obvious but it's amazing how many teachers don't turn to an experienced colleague for help or support. This is almost always down to feeling like they should already know the solution to the problem they have and a fear that they are interrupting someone who is already very busy. Neither of these things are true. All your colleagues will be keen to help you. Don't forget, they are teachers too and love to help through instinct. They will be busy and you'll need to make sure you find the right time to ask for help but don't shy away from asking. By asking for help at the right time, you will be saving time further down the line when a problem can become a bigger issue. The reason it is so important you feel empowered to ask for help is that your colleagues are the most powerful support network you have. Schools are all very different and carry deeply individual contexts. What works in one school may well not work as well in another. What you read in a book (just like this one) or find on the internet may be solid advice but digesting and contextualising the advice can be tricky. By getting the support of your colleagues, you will be able to discuss the realities of your classroom and demographic, allowing you to efficiently and effectively make changes to practice.

Each curriculum subject has a wide-ranging support network, be that in the form of a subject association, online forums or Facebook groups. Too often, teachers are not made aware of these rich pools of support, which often leads to a 'Google roulette' attitude towards acquisition of subject knowledge. It's important to recognise that Google can be an invaluable tool for discovering resources and upskilling ourselves in subject areas we don't feel confident in. However, it is the Wild West in terms of quality and it is very hard to know whether what you are reading is best practice or the right approach. Subject associations spend most of their time and energy on creating accessible resources for teachers to utilise in the classroom, created by experts who know their subject better than anyone.

In the following pages are listed a selection of websites, books and subject associations that should be your 'go to' when looking for subject knowledge support. All links and resources have been collated by National Association of School-Based Teacher Trainers Associate Consultants, who are themselves experts in each subject area. You can access further support from these experts by visiting www.nasbtt.org.uk/tesn.

# Art and design

## Subject associations

National Society for Education in Art and Design – www.nsead.org

Access Art – www.accessart.org.uk

## Recommended reading and useful websites

Eisner, E W (2003) Arts and the Creation of Mind. *Language Arts*, 80(5): 340-4.

Hickman, R (2010) *Why Art Is Taught*. Bristol: Intellect.

Gregory, P, March, C and Tutchell, S (2020) *Mastering Primary Art and Design*. London: Bloomsbury.

Ogier, S (2017) *Teaching Primary Art and Design*. London: Sage.

Ogier, S and Tutchell, S (2021) *Teaching Arts in the Primary Curriculum.* London: Sage.

Tutchell, S (2014) *Young Children as Artists*. Abingdon: Routledge.

Vinney, M (2019) Assessing the Whole Child. In Ogier, S (ed) *A Broad and Balanced Curriculum in the Primary School: Educating the Whole Child* (pp 188-200). London: Sage.

# Computing

## Subject associations

Computing at School (CAS) – www.computingatschool.org.uk

Teach Computing Hubs – https://teachcomputing.org/hubs

## Recommended reading and useful websites

Burrett, M (2016) *Curriculum Basics: Teaching Primary Computing*. London: Bloomsbury.

Computing courses for teachers – https://teachcomputing.org/courses

Hello World (2021) *The Big Book of Computing Pedagogy*. [online] Available at: www.mclibre.org/descargar/docs/revistas/hello-world-books/hello-world-books-the-big-book-of-computing-pedagogy-en-202109.pdf (accessed 12 December 2022).

Hour of Code – https://hourofcode.com/uk

Promoting effective computing pedagogy – https://teachcomputing.org/pedagogy

Teach Computing – https://blog.teachcomputing.org/tag/blog

# Design and technology

## Subject associations

Design and Technology Association (DATA)

## Recommended reading and useful websites

Benson, C and Lawson, S (2017) *Teaching Design and Technology Creatively*. London: Routledge.

Caldwell, H and Pope, S (2019) *STEM in the Primary Curriculum*. London: Sage.

Hope, G (2018) *Mastering Primary Design and Technology*. London: Bloomsbury.

Rutland, M and Turner, A (2020) *Food Education and Food Technology in School Curricula: International Perspectives*. Cham: Springer.

# Geography

## Subject associations

Geographical Association

Royal Geographical Society

## Recommended reading and useful websites

Catling, S and Willy, T (2018) *Understanding and Teaching Primary Geography*. London: Sage.

Tanner, J (2021) Progression in Geographical Fieldwork Experiences. *Primary Geography*, 104: 13–17.

Willy, T (ed) (2019) *Leading Primary Geography: The Essential Handbook for All Teachers*. Sheffield: Geographical Association.

# History

## Subject associations

Historical Association

EuroClio – European Association of History Educators

## Recommended reading and useful websites

Chapman, A (2021) *Knowing History in Schools*. London: UCL Press.

Davies, I (ed) (2017) *Debates in History Teaching*. Oxford: Routledge.

Harris, R, Burn, K and Woolley, M (2014) *The Guided Reader to Teaching and Learning History*. Abingdon: Routledge.

Smith, C, Guillain, A and Noonan, N (2016) *History Through Stories: Teaching Primary History with Storytelling*. Stroud: Hawthorn Press.

# Languages

## Subject associations

Association for Language Learning (ALL)

Research in Primary Languages (RiPL)

## Recommended reading and useful websites

Hood, P (2018) *Teaching Languages Creatively*. London: Routledge.

Jones, J (2006) *Modern Foreign Languages 5–11: A Guide for Teachers*. London: Routledge.

Kirsch, C (2008) *Teaching Foreign Languages in the Primary School*. London: Routledge.

Wright, J and Taylor, A (2016) *The Really Useful Primary Languages Book: Practical Strategies and Ideas for Enjoyable Lessons*. London: Routledge.

# Music

## Subject associations

Music Teachers' Association

Schools Music Association (SMA)

### Recommended reading and useful websites

Atkinson, R (2018) *Mastering Primary Music*. London: Bloomsbury.

Daubney, A (2017) *Teaching Primary Music*. London: Sage.

Minto, D (2009) *Classroom Gems: Games, Ideas and Activities for Primary Music*. Harlow: Pearson.

Stringer, M (2005) *The Music Teacher's Handbook*. London: Faber Music Ltd.

## Physical education

### Subject associations

Association for Physical Education (AfPE)

### Recommended reading and useful websites

Beni, S, Fletcher, T and Ní Chróinín, D (2017) Meaningful Experiences in Physical Education and Youth Sport: A Review of the Literature. *Quest*, 69(3): 291–312.

Griggs, G (2015) *Understanding Primary Physical Education*. London: Routledge.

Howells, K, Carney, A, Castle, N and Little, R (2017) *Mastering Primary Physical Education*. London: Bloomsbury.

Jess, M (2011) Becoming an Effective Primary School Physical Education Teacher. In Amour, K (ed) *Sport Pedagogy: An Introduction for Teaching and Coaching* (pp 271–86). London: Routledge.

Pickard, A and Maude, P (2021) *Teaching Physical Education Creatively*. London: Routledge.

Zachopolou, E, Liukkonen, J, Pickup, I and Tsangaridou, N (2018) *Early Steps Physical Education Curriculum: Theory and Practice for Children Under 8*. Champaign, IL: Human Kinetics.

## Religious education

### Subject associations

National Association of Teachers of Religious Education (NATRE)

The Association of RE Inspectors, Advisers and Consultants (AREIAC)

### Recommended reading and useful websites

Erricker, C, Lowndes, J and Bellchambers, E (2011) *Primary Religious Education: A New Approach*. London: Routledge.

McCreery, E, Palmer, S and Voiels, V (2008) *Teaching Religious Education: Primary and Early Years*. London: Sage.

Teece, G (2012) *The Primary Teacher's Guide to Religious Education*. Witney: Scholastic.

# Reference

Ausubel, D P (1968) *Educational Psychology: A Cognitive View*. New York: Holt, Rinehart and Winston.

Myatt, M and Tomsett, J (2021) *Huh: Curriculum Conversations Between Subject and Senior Leaders*. Woodbridge: John Catt Education Ltd.

# Acronym buster

| Acronym | What does it stand for? |
|---------|--------------------------|
| CPD | Continuing professional development |
| DfE | Department for Education |
| Ofsted | Office for Standards in Education, Children's Services and Skills |
| PPA | Planning, preparation and assessment |
| PE | Physical education |
| RE | Religious education |

# Index

Note: Page numbers in **bold** denote tables.

Printed in the United States
by Baker & Taylor Publisher Services